# JOHN
# MARSHALL

## By James Bradley Thayer

New Introduction by Wallace Mendelsohn
*University of Texas*

DA CAPO PRESS · NEW YORK · 1974

Library of Congress Cataloging in Publication Data

Thayer, James Bradley, 1831-1902.
  John Marshall.

  (Da Capo reprints in American constitutional and
legal history)
  Reprint of the 1901 ed. published by Houghton,
Mifflin, Boston, which was issued as no. 7 in the
Riverside biographical series.
  Bibliography: p.
  1. Marshall, John, 1755-1835. I. Series: The
Riverside biographical series, no. 7.
E302.6.M4T3    1974   347'.73'2634  [B]  76-155923
ISBN 0-306-70287-8

This Da Capo Press edition of
*John Marshall* is an unabridged republication of
the first edition published in Boston and
New York in 1901.

Copyright © 1974 by Da Capo Press, Inc.

A Subsidiary of Plenum Publishing Corporation
227 West 17th Street, New York, New York 10011

# INTRODUCTION

# INTRODUCTION

James Bradley Thayer (1831–1902) was one of the giants of the Harvard Law School in its golden era. His legal career began only after a "strong inclination toward divinity," and the Greek and Latin classics. That his interest in such matters was never entirely suppressed seems evident in his privately printed *A Western Journey with Mr. Emerson* (1884). Yet Thayer was far from a cloistered scholar. He had been a leading practitioner at the Boston bar before he became a teacher of law in 1874—having previously refused a Harvard professorship of English. His tongue and pen were ever ready to promote what seemed to him good causes, e.g. tariff reform, better treatment of the Indians, reform in the granting of corporate franchises.

His professional interest lay primarily in constitutional law and in the law of evidence. In both fields he was, and is, widely recognized as a leading scholar. His great work, *A Preliminary Treatise on Evidence at the Common Law* (1884), led in due course to Wigmore's masterpiece—Wigmore having been his student.

Apart from his technical work, Thayer is now remembered especially for his insistence upon judicial respect for the democratic process. In his view, judges "should keep their hands off of [legislation] wherever it is possible" to do so—by avoiding constitutional issues and deciding cases on other grounds.[1] When alternate grounds are not available, the judicial veto should be exercised, he thought, *only in cases that leave no room for reasonable doubt.*[2]

> This rule recognizes that, having regard to the great, complex, ever-unfolding exigencies of government, much which will seem unconstitutional to one man, or body of men, may reasonably not seem so to another; that the constitution often admits of different interpretations; that there is often a range of choice and judgment; that in such cases the constitution does not impose upon the legislature any one specific opinion, but leaves open this range of choice; and that whatever choice is rational is constitutional.

This view, of course, rests in part upon the Separation of Powers. It rests more heavily on the premise that doubt entails choice—and that in a democracy choice is the province of the people and their *elected* representatives. In short, government by judges is a poor substitute

for government by the people. Obviously
Thayer's thesis (now called the doctrine of
judicial self-restraint) underlies the approach of
the "Harvard Judges"—Holmes, Brandeis, the
Hands and Frankfurter.

Obviously too the old, as well as the new,
activist approaches reject Thayer. Each insists
that judges have a special duty to save us from
our faults by promoting certain interests above
all others. Of course, they disagree as to what
interests deserve this preferred treatment. The
old activists (e.g. Justices Peckham and
Sutherland) favored certain proprietary interests; their modern counterparts (e.g.
Justices Black and Douglas) prefer selected
civil liberties. Each, of course, found its position
plainly prescribed in the written Constitution.
The problem is this: In a democracy, should the
judicial or the political process fix social prior-
ities *when the Constitution leaves room for
doubt?* How free are the people, if they are
denied freedom to make mistakes—that prerogative being reserved for judges? If we rely
upon others to save us, do we repudiate the
moral foundation of freedom, and achieve at
best license?[3]

Thayer's biography of Marshall was designed for popular consumption in commemoration of the hundredth anniversary of Marshall's ascension to the bench. No doubt its author had deep respect for "the great Chief Justice," but could hardly have found him a practitioner of judicial self-restraint. Thus Chapter V—which presents a brief resumé of Thayer's views—quotes a little of Marshall's rhetoric, but says nothing at all of his decisions. Doubtless Thayer had to exercise a great deal of restraint in portraying a judge as aggressive as Marshall. Indeed, there may lie the secret of his success—for he is uncommonly successful. Suppressing his own major "bias," he concentrated on Marshall. And so in large measure—unlike many biographers—he escaped autobiography, and caught what must be the essence of his subject in remarkably few words.

Mr. Justice Holmes had been Thayer's young colleague on the Harvard faculty. A few months before he went to the Supreme Court he too was called upon to commemorate the Marshall centennial. His view of the matter was considerably less restrained than Thayer's. He doubted whether "after Hamilton and the Constitution itself Marshall's work proved more than a strong intellect, a good style, personal ascendancy in his court, courage, justice and the convictions of his party."[4] By thus questioning Marshall's genius, Holmes—a Boston Brahmin—jeopardized his own appointment to the Supreme Court.[5] So deeply had uncritical adulation of Marshall been embedded in our traditions.

If a great judge is one who leaves his mark upon the law—for good or bad, clearly Marshall was one of the elect. Still it is possible with Holmes to question his genius—and indeed the merits of many of his views. Also it is instructive to weigh Marshall's approach in Thayer's scales. To this task we now turn.

## JUDICIAL REVIEW

The traditional view is that Marshall established Judicial Review, "a unique American contribution to the science of government." Surely the principle cannot be attributed to him. The British Privy Council had reviewed colonial legislation.[6] In 1761 James Otis popularized the principle in his famous argument against writs

of assistance.[7] As early as 1782 seven of the
highest judges of Virginia endorsed judicial
review—as did several judges in other states
in the years immediately thereafter.[8] Hamilton
in *The Federalist* (No. 78) presented it to the
American people *as an argument in favor of
ratification of the Constitution.* The first
Congress wrote it unequivocally into Section 25
of the Judiciary Act of 1789, and it was recognized repeatedly as a fact of life by Supreme
Court Justices prior to Marshall's appointment
to the bench.[9] On this matter plainly the "great
Chief Justice" was a Johnny-come-lately.

Does Marshall nevertheless deserve special
honor because his opinion in *Marbury* v.
Madison[10] was the first to strike down an act
of Congress,[11] and thus embalm in precedent
the widely accepted principle of a judicial veto?
Assuming the principle is desirable (many, including Holmes, have had doubts), one may
argue that it survived despite—not because of—
*Marbury* v. *Madison.* Surely that case is a
caricature. It bears the imprint of partisan
politics,[12] and *holds invalid what surely was a
valid act of Congress.* The legislation in question, Section 13 of the Judiciary Act of 1789,

had been enacted by the first Congress, whose membership included James Madison, the "father of the Constitution," and eighteen others who had been members of the Constitutional Convention. It had been approved by President Washington who had been president of the Constitutional Convention. It had been sponsored by a special Senate Judiciary Committee of leading lawyers, five of whose eight (later ten) members had been members of the Constitutional Convention. It had been drafted by the head of that committee, Oliver Ellsworth (soon to become Chief Justice), who as a leading lawyer of the day and the leading legal member of the Convention's five-man Committee of Detail, had in all probability also drafted Article III of the Constitution (with which the Judiciary Act was held to be in conflict). In short, the Judiciary Act was in large measure the product of the Founding Fathers themselves. There is no evidence that any of them, as members of Congress, questioned the provision which Marshall's Court found invalid. Did they not know or understand what they had written a few months earlier at the Constitutional Convention?

xiv           JOHN MARSHALL

Section 13 provided that the Supreme Court "shall have power to issue . . . writs of mandamus, in cases warranted by the principles and usages of law." Doubtless, Ellsworth, Madison, Washington and the others who gave us this measure meant simply what they said; namely, that the court could issue such writs when it properly had jurisdiction in appropriate cases, i.e., only in cases "warranted by the principles and usages of law."[13] Marshall, on the other hand, chose to read Section 13 as authorizing writs in cases *not* within the Court's constitutional jurisdiction. So read, of course, the measure was invalid! In short, Marshall distorted the congressional act and then held the distortion unconstitutional. If the idea of Judicial Review could withstand such abuse—especially when coupled as it was with an attack upon Jefferson—it must have been very tough indeed, and quite able to fend for itself without Marshall's "help."

Obviously in *Marbury* the "great Chief Justice" tried to make a silk purse out of a sow's ear. Why did he not wait for better material? Why the haste? The answer must be that Judicial Review was the Federalist Party's last

hope in its losing struggle with the Jeffersonians.
The engagement began in earnest when Jefferson resigned from Washington's Cabinet and
organized an opposition party. The Federalists
responded with the Alien and Sedition Acts.
The riposte came in the Virginia and Kentucky
Resolutions and Jefferson's great victory at the
polls in 1800. The Federalists replied with the
lame-duck Judiciary Act of 1801—which their
opponents nullified by the Judiciary Act of 1802.
In this Federalist impasse, Marshall evidently
thought Judicial Review would have to be
asserted at once, or never—lest the hated
Jeffersonians destroy everthing that Federalism
had fought for. Jefferson responded with the
Chase Impeachment. This was too much for
Marshall. Obviously moved by the threat, he
wrote Chase an amazing apologia:

> I think the modern doctrine of impeachment should
> yield to an appellate jurisdiction in the legislature.
> A reversal of those legal opinions deemed unsound by
> the legislature would certainly better comport with
> the mildness of our character than [would] a removal
> of the Judge who has rendered them unknowing of
> his fault.[14]

Though he was on the bench for some thirty
years thereafter, neither Marshall nor any of his

colleagues ever again challenged congressional
legislation. This was not for lack of opportunity.[15] Marshall had proposed to his associates that they refuse *on constitutional grounds*
to sit on circuit as required by the Judiciary
Acts of 1802 and 1789. "They agreed that his
views were sound [but] had not the courage to
adopt the heroic course [he] recommended."[16]
Neither did Marshall. Soon another opportunity
arose in *Stuart* v. *Laird*.[17] Again no judge
ventured to express the Court's conviction that
the legislation was unconstitutional (Marshall
did not participate in the decision because he
had heard the case—and avoided the issue—on
circuit). The problem was "solved" by asserting
that "practice and acquiescence. . .has fixed"
the meaning of the Constitution in favor of the
legislation. The *written* words, it would seem,
had been amended by prescription. This is
difficult to reconcile with *Marbury*. There (only
six days earlier) Marshall had said the basic
premise of a written constitution must be that
its terms shall be enforced *as written*—such
enforcement being the special function of judges.

For one who concentrates on the words of
judicial opinions, the legacy of these two cases

at best is fuzzy. For the essence of what was said in one was undermined in the other. To one who discounts words for deeds, the legacy is quite clear. Marshall and his colleagues were prepared to strike down an innocuous measure (Section 13 of the Judiciary Act of 1789) when the immediate effect would be a victory for a popular president and the dominant political party. They were not prepared to veto major legislation *which they deemed invalid* when the effect would seriously affront the prevailing power structure. Thus the operational meaning of *Marbury* and *Laird*, it would seem, is this: the Court will not attempt to block the major political forces of the day. Surely this is incompatible with the basic rationale of Judicial Review as a check upon a wayward Congress and President.

The Court did not again interfere with national legislation until more than 50 years later in *Dred Scott's* case.[18] Surely that catastrophe stands on its own feet, quite independent of *Marbury* v. *Madison*. Indeed Taney's fault in *Dred Scott* was that he had not learned the *Marbury-Laird* lesson; namely, that a court does well to avoid interference with dominant

political forces. And so the wonder is that
Judicial Review could have survived at all after
the blatantly contrived *Marbury* and the
disaster of *Dred Scott*. That it did survive, and
indeed thrive after the Civil War, suggests it
did so—Marshall and Taney notwithstanding—
because it served a new post-bellum need in
the American political system.[19]

In some of its aspects, Judicial Review of
state acts entails considerations quite different
from those involved in review of national affairs.
The great lesson of the Articles of Confederation
was that the whole cannot survive at the mercy
of its parts. There was virtually unanimous
agreement in the Constitutional Convention on
the need for national control of the states. The
problem was what form it should take. The
Virginia Plan proposed a congressional veto of
state measures "contravening. . .the articles of
union, or any treaties subsisting under the
authority of the union." The New Jersey Plan
proposed instead an executive-military veto "to
enforce and compel an obedience" to the acts
and treaties of the United States. While some
traces of each of these will be found in the
Constitution, the basic solution was the

Supremacy Clause and the judicial veto.[20] Section 25 of the Judiciary Act of 1789, of course, and Marshall's crucial opinion in *Cohens* v. *Virginia* (1821) implemented this approach.

Here, then, again Marshall was not an innovator. But how wisely, and to what ends, did he use the veto thus given him? For this power, unlike that with respect to national measures, he used frequently and with striking results.

## VESTED RIGHTS

Years ago Professor Corwin found the basic premise of early American constitutional law in the doctrine of vested rights. Supported by those who deemed property fundamental, it was calculated in its purest form to nullify any law impairing established proprietary interests.[21] It finds classic expression in *Fletcher* v. *Peck*[22] and *Dartmouth College* v. *Woodward*.[23] For want of a better constitutional peg, these cases were hung on the Contract Clause.[24] That provision quite plainly had been put into the Constitution to prevent the states from easing the

burdens of debtors (as they had in the past) by
stay laws or related measures. Even Marshall
acknowledged that a case like *Dartmouth* was
"not in the mind of the [Constitutional] Convention" when it adopted the Contract Clause[25]
(he might well have said the same of *Fletcher)*.
Still less must it have been contemplated by
those who ratified the Constitution. Marshall
insisted, however, that *Dartmouth* and *Fletcher*
came within the letter of the Contract Clause
whatever its spirit.[26]

As Thayer indicates—and what he says is
even more clearly settled now—the Contract
Clause doctrine of vested rights has been
qualified virtually out of existence. The reason
is obvious. It rests on the untenable premise
that a state in covenants with private persons may barter away substantial parts of its
power to govern. More broadly it seems vul-
nerable also in its assumption that proprietary
values are—or were—virtually supreme in
American culture.[27]

However unacceptable the sovereignty of
vested rights may seem today, Marshall
enthusiasts insist it served the infant American
economy well—by putting corporate charters

(contracts) beyond the meddlesome control of legislatures. This is highly questionable. For as Mr. Justice Story observed in *Dartmouth*, states could keep the right to meddle, i.e., protect the public, by including as part of the corporate charter itself the power to alter, amend, or revoke. This of course immediately became common practice, and indeed was not unknown before the *Dartmouth* decision.[28] In any event, here again Marshall deserves no major credit for invention. His opinion in *Fletcher* (the first contract case) had been previewed in a widely circulated opinion Hamilton had written years earlier as a private lawyer advising his clients in the same Yazoo controversy.[29]

Entirely apart from their initial or ultimate value, *Fletcher* and *Dartmouth*, like *Marbury*, reveal how far Marshall was prepared to stretch amenities to achieve his peculiar ends. *Dartmouth* qualified the American Revolution by holding that for some purposes George III still ruled in America *ad infinitum*. The point is, that even if vested rights generally must be elevated as high as Marshall insisted, there was little reason for giving that status indiscriminately to pre-revolutionary royal charter claims.

Thomas Jefferson took an even broader view in his famous letter to Governor Plumer (July 21, 1819) supporting the state's power to alter Dartmouth's charter:

> The idea that institutions established for the use of the nation cannot be touched nor modified, even to make them answer their end, because of rights gratuitously supposed in those employed to manage them in trust for the public, may perhaps be a salutary provision against the abuses of a monarch, but is most absurd against the nation itself. Yet our lawyers and priests generally inculcate this doctrine, and suppose that preceding generations held the earth more freely than we do; had a right to impose laws on us, unalterable by ourselves, and that we, in like manner, can make laws and impose burthens on future generations, which they will have no right to alter; in fine, that the earth belongs to the dead and not the living.

As though tacitly recognizing a weakness in *Dartmouth*, some Marshall supporters suggest that decision was designed primarily, if indirectly, for the benefit of American business corporation charters—little Dartmouth College being simply a convenient vehicle.

*Fletcher* grew out of a malodorous bit of private enterprise in public land. A northern syndicate bribed most members of the Georgia legislature and thus obtained 35 million acres of public domain for less than two cents per acre. The people of Georgia immediately discovered the fraud and elected a new legislature which repealed the tainted transaction. Fletcher, having bought some of the land from successors of the syndicate, challenged the repeal law as a violation of Georgia's original "contract." Marshall and his Court sustained the challenge.

In retrospect the case seems riddled with difficulties. First is the problem of whether Marshall should have participated in deciding it. His sympathetic biographer, Beveridge, makes the point apparently without realizing that he does so:

> Marshall was profoundly interested in the stability of contractual obligations. The repudiation of these by the Legislature of Virginia had powerfully and permanently influenced his views upon this subject. Also, Marshall's own title to part of the Fairfax estate had more than once been in jeopardy. At that very moment a suit affecting the title of his brother to certain Fairfax lands was pending in Virginia courts. ...No man in America, therefore, could have followed with deeper anxiety the [Yazoo] controversy than did John Marshall.[30]

It is questionable, indeed, whether even the Court should have heard the case. For, as Mr. Justice Johnson recognized in a separate opinion, it reeked of collusion. Modern research seems to establish beyond doubt that Johnson's suspicions were well founded and based on evidence plainly in view.[31]

Marshall seems to have been untroubled by these problems. In his opinion the fraudulent grant was a covenant with continuing obligations which the Contract Clause protected (after the property had passed into the hands of innocent purchasers). That this view of the grant was not inevitable is demonstrated in Mr. Justice Johnson's separate opinion—a grant is a completed transaction that entails no further obligations to which the Contract Clause could apply.

About three months before the *Fletcher* case was initiated, James Madison, Albert Gallatin, and Levi Lincoln after a thorough investigation of the whole Yazoo problem reported to Congress that:

> Under all the circumstances which may affect the case. . .the title of the claimants cannot be supported. [Yet] the interest of the United States, the tran-

quility of those who thereafter may inhabit that
territory, and various equitable considerations. . .
render it expedient to enter into a compromise on
reasonable terms.[32]

Marshall's view, of course, contradicted the
findings of that eminent presidential commission.
His point that purchase by an innocent third
party cuts off the rights of the defrauded initial
owner is sound common law *with respect to
private persons*. Whether it was, or is, applicable in the case of a defrauded "sovereign," and
whether it is necessarily embedded in the Constitution, is at least questionable.[33]

Waiving these difficulties, however, only
presents a greater one. Was Fletcher in fact
an innocent purchaser unaware of the fraud that
tainted the whole transaction? The evidence
strongly indicates that he was not. It seems
unlikely that, as a seasoned land speculator, he
would be innocent of all knowledge of the
greatest land scandal in American history
several years after it had become public
knowledge. This point need not be pursued,
however, for the deed which conveyed the land
to him contained a most unusual warranty;
namely, that "title. . .has been in no way con-

stitutionally or legally impaired by virtue of
any subsequent act of any subsequent legislature
of the state of Georgia."[34] Obviously this provision was designed to make a case for testing
the repeal law (this is a small part of the
collusion point). Is it conceivable that a party
to such a warranty had no knowledge of the
repeal *and the reasons for it?*

Conservative tradition holds that by putting
the sanctity of "contracts" above other considerations of ethics and public welfare, Marshall
and his colleagues promoted economic stability.
Would it not be at least equally relevant to suggest that *Fletcher* encouraged the flagrant cor-
ruption of state politics and the reckless waste of
natural resources that marked the nineteenth
century? Surely judicial "protection" of fraud
in the Yazoo land scandal helped pave the way
for the Robber Barons and their Great
Barbecue at the expense of the American
people. And what of the instability generated by
a court decision permitting a state and its people
to be deprived of their property through fraud?
Finally why is it more unsettling for a legislature to upset established rights than for a

court to do so, as in *Gibbons* v. *Ogden* (discussed below)?

The broad implications of these contract decisions is best revealed in the *Charles River Bridge* case.[35] In 1785, when Boston and Charlestown were small towns on opposite sides of the Charles River, the State gave a private company the right to build and operate an inter-city toll bridge. As population grew the value of the toll rights increased, and a single bridge became inadequate for the growing traffic. When the state authorized a competing bridge in 1828, the owners of the original facility objected on Contract Clause grounds. In a dissenting opinion, Mr. Justice Story voted to sustain their view:

> I stand upon the old law established more than three centuries ago. . .in resisting any such encroachments upon the rights and liberties of the citizens, secured by public grant. I will not consent to shake their title deeds by any speculative niceties or novelties.

The Court in an opinion by Chief Justice Taney—formerly "prime minister" of the Jackson Administration—took a quite different position:

> While the rights of property are sacredly guarded,
> we must not forget that the community also have
> rights, and that the happiness and well-being of
> every citizen depends on their faithful preservation.

Then, looking ahead, he observed that, if the
old charter blocked a new bridge, then old
turnpike charters would block the new canals
and railroads. Thus the country would

> be thrown back to the improvements of the last
> century, and obliged to stand still, until the claims
> of the old turnpike corporations shall be satisfied;
> and they shall consent to permit these states to avail
> themselves of the lights of modern science, and to
> partake of the benefit of those improvements which
> are now adding to the wealth and prosperity, and
> the convenience and comfort, of every part of the
> civilized world. . . . [I]f such a right of property exists,
> we have no lights to guide us in marking out its
> extent, unless, indeed, we resort to the feudal grants,
> and to the exclusive rights of ferries, by prescription,
> between towns; and are prepared to decide that when
> a turnpike road from one town to another has been
> made, no railroad or canal, between these two points,
> could afterwards be established.

Where Marshall and Story apparently saw a
clash between private property and anarchy,
others could see—in all the contract cases—a
clash between private property and other no

less important social interests. Thayer's doctrine means that the resolution of such conflicts is essentially a legislative function, to be disturbed by judges only in cases beyond the realm of rational doubt.

## DEMOCRACY

In a few striking sentences, Marshall's great admirer and leading biographer summarized what is implicit in *Marbury* and the contract cases:

> [The "great Chief Justice" was] obsessed with an almost religious devotion to the rights of property, to steady government by "the rich, the wise and the good". . .
>
> In short [he] had become the personification of the reaction against popular government that followed the French Revolution. . . .
>
> The conclusion of his early manhood—. . .that the people, left to themselves, are not capable of self-government—had now become a profound moral belief.[36]

These sound Federalist doctrines expressed the conventional wisdom of the day—*inherited from the old-world's class-oriented, property-governed social ethos.* As all good conservatives in the early nineteenth century knew, government had always been, and must be, in the hands of a wealthy few sustained against the masses by the whole weight of social, religious, economic and political convention. To tamper with vested rights—proprietarian, religious, or whatever— was to destroy the cement that had always bound the classes together in a cohesive social union. The repudiation of this "old unity" was the essence of the French Revolution and what Jefferson called his "revolution at the polls" in 1800. Small wonder then that Marshall considered Jefferson an "absolute terrorist."[37] What irony that the one became Chief Justice just when the other became President—that old-world fears were entrenched in the judiciary when new-world ideals took over Congress and the White House.

## NATIONALISM

John Marshall was at his best—and as it developed, most forward looking—in cases defining the scope of national power and its effect upon the states. The reason is plain. Here his genius fed not on *European dogmas*, but on new-world experience, i.e., the chaos of state anarchy under the Articles of Confederation.

*McCulloch* v. *Maryland*,[38] as Thayer indicates, is Marshall's major opus. Again drawing heavily upon Hamilton,[39] he developed the principle of implied national power, specifically the power to charter a bank. Then, borrowing from Daniel Webster's brief—"the power to tax involves the power to destroy,"— he held federal functions (here banking) immune by virtue of the Supremacy Clause[40] from state reserved power to tax. While Marshall had help from others in evolving these doctrines, he expressed them in a manner magnificently his own. If the style is the man, it is also often the decision.

The other major case in this area is *Gibbons* v. *Ogden*.[41] New York had given Fulton (inventor of the steamboat) a patent, i.e., exclusive steamboat rights on the Hudson River in New York for a limited time. This had become an impediment to the free flow of traffic, and was highly unpopular. But because of the *Fletcher* doctrine of vested rights, New York

felt it could not repeal its "mistake."[42] Hence
*Gibbons* v. *Ogden* which challenged the New
York grant as an invalid state intrusion upon
national interests. Marshall upheld the challenge. First, with help from Webster's brief, he
gave an expansive interpretation of the nation's
commerce power—so expansive indeed one sus-
pects he had some special vision extending into
the twentieth century. Then he strongly commended, and so gave the weight of his position,
to Webster's argument that this broad power
was exclusive (i.e., that it automatically
invalidated any state law within its compass).
Yet in the end he turned his decision on the
milder view that the New York law was invalid
because in conflict with an existing federal
statute. This "self-restraint," this apparent
doubt as to the validity of an extreme position
which he obviously favored, is most
unusual—perhaps unique—in Marshall's jurisprudence.

One crucial test of a court decision is to judge
its consequences against those that might be
expected from an opposite decision. The judg-
ments that Marshall rejected in *McCulloch* and
in *Gibbons* would have reinstated the anarchy

of the Articles of Confederation—leaving the states as free as before to block the operations of the nation and the free flow of national intercourse. As Mr. Justice Frankfurter observed: Marshall "was on guard against every tendency to continue treating the new Union as though it were the old Confederation."

## FROM MARSHALL TO THAYER

How might a Thayer-oriented judge—an early Brandeis or Hand—have disposed of these cases? *Marbury* required no more than a single sentence: "Neither party being a state, ambassador, minister, or consul (see Constitution, Article III, Section 2), the case is dismissed for want of original jurisdiction." This is precisely Marshall's *result* unadorned by the attack on Jefferson and the remarks on Judicial Review. Surely it would neither have hindered nor helped the judge-veto principle which (as we have seen) was firmly established in *The Federalist*, in Section 25 of the Judiciary Act, in the remarks and assumptions of several earlier Supreme Court opinions, as well as in state practice.

Surely a responsible judge (having no corporation fish to fry) could have disagreed with
the *Dartmouth* decision. Would he have been
"wrong" in holding that—whatever the intra-
mural meaning of the Contract Clause—*in view
of the American Revolution* it did not apply to
pre 1776 royal charters calculated to impede the
management of American educational affairs
after the Declaration of Independence? An
opinion couched in such narrow terms could not
have prejudiced the future development of the
Contract Clause. Meanwhile, it would have left
the people of New Hampshire free to manage
their educational affairs without royal interference.[43]

*Fletcher* might well have been dismissed as a
feigned or collusive action. Even if that difficulty were to be bypassed, a judge need only
have said: "Assuming *but not deciding* that the
Contract Clause applies in a case like this, and
assuming [with Marshall] that it embodies the
innocent-purchaser doctrine of the common law,
Fletcher's claims must be denied because he has
not established his innocence. Indeed all the
evidence looks in the opposite direction." Or,
going all the way, a judge might well have left

the states unfettered in the *Fletcher* context by holding the Contract Clause inapplicable for reasons given in Mr. Justice Johnson's separate opinion. While this approach goes much farther than the other two, it seems in accord with both the historic purpose and the language of the Contract Clause. Moreover, as indicated above, it comes very close *in effect* to the meaning ultimately found in the contract provision anyway. Finally none of the three suggested approaches to *Fletcher* would have embarrassed —as Marshall's decision did—congressional settlement of the whole Yazoo problem (which of course is how it was finally settled in any event).

Had the Thayer-oriented view prevailed in *Fletcher* (see above), it is not likely that *Gibbons* v. *Ogden* would ever have arisen. The pressure upon the New York legislature to repeal the hated steamboat "monopoly" was great. Only the unfortunate *Fletcher* decision seems to have stood in the way.[44] In any event, apart from Marshall's extravagant dicta, *Gibbons* itself, as above suggested, is a model of restraint, invalidating *on a narrower rather than a broader ground* an invidious state intrusion upon national affairs.

Of course, Thayer's approach would leave the national bank intact, as *McCulloch* did. It would not in the least have detracted from the great principle of implied powers as earlier enunciated by Hamilton and endorsed by two Congresses and two Presidents—Washington and Madison, no less. But surely instead of striking expansively with Marshall at *all* state taxes on federal functions, the Thayer approach would have focused on the discriminatory nature of the tax in question. This would have spared the future a plague of trouble. As Paul Freund puts it:

> That the power to tax is the power to destroy. . . that the power over Congress among the several states is exclusively lodged in Congress. . .were doctrines going beyond the necessities of the case or problem, doctrines which plagued constitutional law for a long time, because they could not contain the counterpressures from state interests that had been slighted in [Marshall's] formulas. . . . [The] momentum of doctrine shot beyond its mark, and other generations were obliged to retrace some giant steps in order to follow a viable course.[45]

As suggested above, Marshall overshot even more drastically in the Contract Clause cases.

Overshooting, i.e., the making of doubtful,

unnecessary or premature constitutional com-
mitments, is the curse of judicial activism. It
blocks, or at least impedes, the solution of social
problems by the democratic process. For the
greater the activism of the judge, the less is
the freedom and responsibility of the people to
govern themselves. Thayer did not suggest that
Judicial Review should be abandoned; it was
after all an established part of our constitutional
system. But he recognized that constitutional
standards for judicial judgment are often vague;
that courts have very limited capacity to find
and assess all of the data necessary for an informed judgment on the broad social issues
behind the immediate claims of litigants; that
judicial intervention in such matters necessarily
is sporadic and haphazard; that judges have no
unique immunity from mistakes; and that error
in upholding legislation can be corrected by the
people far more readily than error raised to the
status of a constitutional limitation. Moreover
history does to all judges what it did to Marshall.
It reworks decisions that do not conform with
the needs of the community. For all these
reasons Thayer and his disciples insist upon
economy in the exercise of the judicial veto.

How could Marshall have become a folk-hero being so out of tune with American ideals as to hate democracy, consider Jefferson a "terrorist," and make vested interests all but sovereign (at least vis-a-vis legislation)? If, as suggested, his efforts tended to perpetuate decadent, old-world dogmas in the new land of liberty, how does one explain his popular repute as a great judge? For one thing, his majestic, premise-obscuring rhetoric tends to hide the sometimes shabby side of the claims that his decisions protected. More important, he served well the conservative interests of his day—and for a long time it was conservatives who wrote history books. Generations of eulogy by the comfortable classes have left their mark. Few have ventured with Holmes to question Marshall's genius.

Far more, however, is involved than a majestic style or snowballing adulation. Specialization and division of labor have bound us all together in a close web of economic interdependence. Our world has so changed since the Civil War that Marshall's nationalism, stripped of its immediate mercantile implications, has come of age. (His contract decisions are long since dead.) What defied the aspirations of the common man in a localized, agrarian economy has become indispensable to his welfare in a modern industrial setting. Virtually all liberal reform measures since the Square Deal are based on visions of national authority adumbrated in Marshall's rhetoric—particularly in *Gibbons* and *McCulloch*. Having built Marshall up so high for so long, conservatives apparently now have no stomach for attacking him. Others have no cause to do so. Quite the contrary! Marshall's expansive nationalism has become a bulwark of modern liberalism. Finally, since 1936 "his" veto has been limited all but exclusively to the protection of civil liberty.[46]

FOOTNOTES

[1] This principle is spelled out in the opinion of Mr. Justice Brandeis in *Ashwander* v. *TVA*, 297 U.S. 288 (1936).

[2] James Bradley Thayer, "The Origin and Scope of the American Doctrine of Constitutional Law," *Harvard Law Review*, 7 (1893), 129.

[3] Sympathetic accounts of the new activism will be found in Charles Black, *The People and the Court* (New York: The Macmillan Company, 1960) and Eugene Rostow, *The Sovereign Prerogative* (New Haven: Yale University Press, 1962). With respect to the old activism, see Arthur T. Hadley, "The Consitutional Position of Property in America," *The Independent*, 64 (1908), 834.

[4] Oliver Wendell Holmes, Jr., Collected Legal Papers (New York: Harcourt, Brace and Company, 1920), p. 269.

[5] "Oliver Wendell Holmes," Dictionary of American Biography (New York: Charles Scribner's Sons, 1944) XXI, Supp. 1, p. 422.

[6] Arthur E. Sutherland, *Constitutionalism in America* (New York: Blaisdell Publishing Co., 1965), p. 323.

[7] *Ibid.*

[8] *Commonwealth* v. *Caton*, 4 Call. (Va.) 5 (1782). Noel T. Dowling, *Cases on Constitutional Law* (Brooklyn: The Foundation Pres, Inc., 5th ed., 1954), pp. 70 et. seq.

[9] *Ibid.*

[10] 1 Cranch 137 (1803).

[11] But see *Haybern's Case*, 2 Dallas 409 (1792).

[12] See Robert G. McCloskey, *The American Supreme Court* (Chicago: The University of Chicago Press, 1960), pp. 40–44.

[13] See also the "exceptions" clause in Article III, Sec. 2, par. 2, of the Constitution.

[14] Albert J. Beveridge, *The Life of John Marshall* (Boston: Houghton Mifflin Company, 1916), Vol. 3, p. 117.

[15] *Id.*, Vol. IV, pp. 117–119.

[16] *Id.*, Vol. III, p. 122.

[17] 1 Cranch 299 (1803), and *ibid*.

[18] *Dred Scott* v. *Sanford*, 19 Howard 393 (1857).

[19] Perhaps a paralysis of the party system after 1865 created a vacuum in our national policy-making processes which invited judicial intervention. See W. Mendelson, "The Politics of Judicial Supremacy," *The Journal of Law and Economics*, 4 (1961), 175.

[20] Andrew C. McLaughlin, *A Constitutional History of the United States* (New York: D. Appleton-Century Company, 1936), pp. 181–185.

[21] Edward S. Corwin, "The Basic Doctrine of American Constitutional Law," *Michigan Law Review* 12 (1914), 255.

[22] 6 Cranch 87 (1810).

[23] 4 Wheaton 518 (1819).

[24] The Constitution in Article 1, Sec. 10 provides: "No state shall. . .pass any. . .law impairing the obligation of contracts. . . ."

[25] See the *Dartmouth College Case*, 4 Wheaton 518 (1819).

[26] In *Brown* v. *Maryland*, 12 Wheaton 419 (1827), Marshall looked beyond the letter to the spirit to strike down a state tax.

[27] No doubt property was very high in the value system of the then moribund Federalist Party.

[28] *Wales* v. *Stetson*, 2 Mass. 143 (1806).

[29] C. Peter Magrath, *Yazoo* (Providence: Brown University Press, 1966), pp. 21–24.

[30] *Op. cit.*, Vol. III, p. 582.

[31] Magrath, *op. cit.*, p. 54.

[32] *American State Papers*, Public Lands, Vol. I, p. 134. (Feb. 14, 1803).

[33] ". . .there can be no irrepealable contract in a conveyance . . .in disregard of a public trust. . . ." *Illinois Central Rd.* v. *Illinois*, 146 U.S. 387 (1892).

[34] Quoted in *Fletcher* v. *Peck*, 6 Cranch 87 (1810).

[35] 11 Peters 420 (1837). In *Providence Bank* v. *Billings*, 4 Peters 514 (1830), Marshall had "anticipated" Taney's position by refusing to imply a covenant against taxation.

[36] Beveridge, *op. cit.*, Vol. IV, pp. 4, 488.

[37] Charles Warren, *The Supreme Court in United States History* (Boston: Little, Brown and Company, 1937), pp. 183–184.

[38] 4 Wheaton 316 (1819).

[39] See Hamilton's "Opinion on the Constitutionality of the Bank," Feb. 23, 1791. *The Works of Alexander Hamilton*, H. C. Lodge, ed. (New York: G. P. Putnam's Sons, 1904) Vol. III, p. 450.

[40] Constitution, Article VI, par. 2.

[41] 9 Wheaton 1 (1824).

[42] See Wallace Mendelson, "New Light on *Fletcher* v. *Peck* and *Gibbons* v. *Ogden*," Yale Law Journal, 58 (1949), 567.

[43] What would Marshall's decision have been if Dartmouth had been chartered to teach "the divine right of kings"?

[44] Mendelson, *loc. cit.*, note 42, above.

[45] "New Vistas in Constitutional Law," *University of Pennsylvania Law Review*, 112 (1964), 631, 639.

[46] The only substantial exception is its continuing use to protect the national market from state interference which after all was the basic problem that led to the Constitutional Convention. A classic modern case is *Southern Pacific Co.* v. *Arizona*, 325 U.S. 761 (1945).

BIBLIOGRAPHY

## JAMES BRADLEY THAYER

Ames, J. B., Gray, J. C., Smith, J., and Williston, S. "James Bradley Thayer," *Harvard Law Review*, 15 (1902), 599–607.

Anon. "James Bradley Thayer," *American Law Review*, 36 (1902), 248.

Greenough, C. P. "Memoir of James Bradley Thayer," *Massachusetts Historical Society*, Jan.–Mar. 1919, pp. 133–138.

Hall, J. P. "James Bradley Thayer" in Lewis, W. D. (ed.). *Great American Lawyers* Vol. VIII Philadelphia: The John C. Winston Company, 1907–1909.

Thayer, J. B. *A Preliminary Treatise On Evidence At The Common Law.* Boston: Little, Brown & Co., 1898.

Thayer, J. B. *Cases on Constitutional Law.* Cambridge: C. W. Sever and Company, 1895.

Thayer, J. B. *Legal Essays.* Cambridge: Harvard University Press, 1927.

Thayer, J. B. *Select Cases On Evidence At Common Law.* Cambridge: C. W. Sever and Company, 1900.


## JOHN MARSHALL

Beveridge, A. J. *The Life of John Marshall*, 4 vols. Boston: Houghton Mifflin Company, 1916–1919.

Boyd, J. P. "Thomas Jefferson's Empire of Liberty," *Virginia Quarterly Review*, 24 (1948), 538–554.

Corwin, E. S. *John Marshall and The Constitution.* New Haven: Yale University Press, 1919.

Dillon, J. M. *John Marshall, Complete Constitutional Decisions.* Chicago: Callaghan and Company, 1903.

Elliot, J. (ed.). *The Debates In The Several State Conventions On The Adoption Of The Federal Constitution.* Vol. III. Philadelphia: J. P. Lippincott and Company, 1836.

Frankfurter, F. "John Marshall And The Judicial Function," *Harvard Law Review,* 69 (1955), 217–238.

Marshall, J. *The Life Of George Washington.* Philadelphia: C. P. Wayne, 1804–1807.

Roche, J. P. *The Writings Of John Marshall.* Indianapolis: The Bobbs-Merrill Company, Inc., 1967.

Servies, J. A. *A Bibliography of John Marshall.* Washington: United States Commission For the Celebration Of The Two Hundredth Anniversary Of The Birth Of John Marshall, 1956.

Symposium, "Chief Justice Marshall," *University of Pensylvania Law Review,* 104 (1955), 1–68.

The Riverside Biographical Series

NUMBER 7

# JOHN MARSHALL

BY

JAMES BRADLEY THAYER

# JOHN MARSHALL

BY

JAMES BRADLEY THAYER

BOSTON AND NEW YORK
HOUGHTON, MIFFLIN AND COMPANY
The Riverside Press, Cambridge
1901

## PREFATORY NOTE

THE writer has drawn with entire freedom from an address delivered by him at Cambridge on February 4, 1901, before the Harvard Law School and the Bar Association of the City of Boston, and from an article on John Marshall in the Atlantic Monthly for March, 1901.            J. B. T.

CAMBRIDGE, March 30, 1901.

# CONTENTS

*The portrait is from a miniature by St. Mémin.*

# JOHN MARSHALL

## CHAPTER I

### HIS LIFE BEFORE BECOMING CHIEF JUSTICE; HIS PERSONAL CHARACTERISTICS

In beginning his " Life of Washington," Chief Justice Marshall states that Washington was born in 1732, "near the banks of the Potowmac," in Westmoreland County, Virginia; mentions his employment by Lord Fairfax, the proprietor of the Northern Neck, as surveyor of his estates in the western part of that region; and adds that, in the performance of these duties, " he acquired that information respecting vacant lands, and formed those opinions concerning their future value, which afterwards contributed greatly to the increase of his private fortune."

Thomas Marshall, the father of the Chief Justice, two years older than Washington, was also born in Westmoreland County, was a schoolmate of Washington, served with him both as surveyor of the Fairfax estates, and soon afterwards, as an officer in the French and Indian wars; and he, too, as time passed, found like advantage from his experience as a surveyor.

In 1753, Thomas Marshall was made agent of Lord Fairfax in the management of his estates. In the next year, he married Mary Isham Keith, daughter of a Scotch clergyman, whose wife was a descendant of William Randolph, of Turkey Island, the ancestor of the famous Virginia family of that name. Their son, John Marshall, the oldest of fifteen children, was born on September 24, 1755, in what was afterwards Fauquier County, at a little settlement then known as Germantown, — now Midland, on the Southern Railroad, a few miles south of Manassas. That was the year of Braddock's defeat, and Thomas Marshall, like Washington, was in the service, as an officer.

In Marshall's early childhood, his father's household, situated in a frontier county, must have been agitated with the dreadful rumors, anxieties, and terrors of the troubles with the French and Indians. " So late," he tells us in the " Life of Washington," " as the year 1756, the Blue Ridge was the northwestern frontier; and [Virginia] found immense difficulty in completing a single regiment to protect the inhabitants from the horrors of the scalping-knife, and the still greater horrors of being led into captivity by savages who added terrors to death by the manner of inflicting it." It was not until two years later that the capture of Fort Duquesne relieved Virginia from the frightful ravages that laid waste the region just west of the Blue Ridge.

When John Marshall was ten years old or more, his father left the level country and poor soil of eastern Fauquier, for the higher and more fertile region in the western part of the county, just under the Blue Ridge. At Midland all they can show you now, relating to Marshall, is a small, rude heap

of bricks and rubbish, — what is left of
the house where he was born ; and children
on the farm reach out to you a handful of
the bullets with which that sacred spot
and the whole region were thickly sown,
before a generation had passed, after his
death.

Marshall's education was got from his
father, from such teachers as the neighbor-
hood furnished, and, for about a year, at a
school in Westmoreland County, where his
father and George Washington had attended, and where James Monroe was his
own schoolmate. But most he owed to his
father, — a man of good stock, of enterprise, experience, strong character and sense,
himself of no mean education, — who, personally, took great pains with the training of
his children. Marshall admired his father,
and declared him to be a far abler man than
any of his sons. From him and the teachers
provided for him his son got a good knowledge
of English history, literature, and poetry, and
a fair acquaintance with the classics.

All Marshall's later youth was passed in

the mountain region of Fauquier County, under the Blue Ridge. Judge Story declared that it was to the hardy, athletic habits of his youth among the mountains, operating, we may well conjecture, upon a happy physical inheritance, "that he probably owed that robust and vigorous constitution which carried him almost to the close of his life with the freshness and firmness of manhood."

The house that Marshall's father built at Oakhill is still standing, an unpretending, small, frame building, having connected with it now, as a part of it, another house built by Marshall's son Thomas. At one time the farm comprised an estate of six thousand acres.[1] Since 1865 it has passed out of the hands of the family. It is beautifully placed on high, rolling ground, looking over a great stretch of fertile country, and along the chain of the Blue Ridge, close by. To this

[1] The Chief Justice seems to have inherited and accumulated a considerable estate. By his will he gave to each of his grandsons named John a thousand acres of land. *The Green Bag*, viii. 4. He also had been a surveyor. *Ib.* 480.

region, where his children and kindred lived, about a hundred miles from Richmond, Marshall delighted to resort in the summer, all his life long. In the autumn of 1807, after the Burr trial, he writes to a friend, "The day after the commitment of Colonel Burr for a misdemeanor, I galloped to the mountains." " I am on the wing," he tells Judge Story in 1828, " for my friends in the upper country, where I shall find rest and dear friends, occupied more with their farms than with party politics."

When Marshall was about eighteen years old he began to study Blackstone ; but he quickly dropped it, for the troubles with Great Britain thickened, and, like his neighbors, he prepared for fighting.

He seems to have found a copy of Blackstone in his father's house, as he had found there much other sterling English literature. It was then a new book, but already famous. Published in England in 1765–69, a thousand copies had been taken in this country ; [1] and just now the first American edition was

[1] Hammond's Blackstone, vol. i., pp. viii. **xxv.**

out (Philadelphia, 1771–72), in which the list of subscribers, headed by the name of "John Adams, barrister at law, Boston," had also that of "Captain Thomas Marshall, Clerk of Dunmore County." Dunmore County, now Shenandoah, was then a very new county, just over the Blue Ridge from Fauquier; and it is believed that there was but one Captain Thomas Marshall in those parts.

The earliest personal description of Marshall that we have belongs to this period. It is preserved in Horace Binney's admirable address at Philadelphia, after Marshall's death. He gives it from the pen of an eyewitness, a "venerable kinsman" of Marshall. News had come, in May, 1775, of the fighting at Concord and Lexington. The account shows us the youth, as lieutenant, drilling a company of soldiers in Fauquier County : —

"He was about six feet high, straight, and rather slender, of dark complexion, showing little if any rosy red, yet good health, the outline of the face nearly a cir-

cle, and within that, eyes dark to blackness,[1]
strong and penetrating, beaming with intelligence and good nature; an upright forehead, rather low, was terminated in a horizontal line by a mass of raven-black hair, of
unusual thickness and strength. The features of the face were in harmony with this
outline, and the temples fully developed.
The result of this combination was interesting and very agreeable. The body and
limbs indicated agility rather than strength,
in which, however, he was by no means de-
ficient. He wore a purple or pale blue
hunting-shirt, and trousers of the same material fringed with white. A round black
hat, mounted with the buck's tail for a cock-
ade, crowned the figure and the man. He
went through the manual exercise by word
and motion, deliberately pronounced and
performed in the presence of the company,
before he required the men to imitate him;
and then proceeded to exercise them with
the most perfect temper. . . .

[1] Marshall's eyes are often spoken of as black. In
fact, they were brown.

" After a few lessons the company were dismissed, and informed that if they wished to hear more about the war, and would form a circle about him, he would tell them what he understood about it. The circle was formed, and he addressed the company for something like an hour. He then challenged an acquaintance to a game of quoits, and they closed the day with foot-races and other athletic exercises, at which there was no betting."

" This," adds Mr. Binney, " is a portrait, to which in simplicity, gayety of heart, and manliness of spirit, in everything but the symbols of the youthful soldier, and one or two of those lineaments which the hand of time, however gentle, changes and perhaps improves, he never lost his resemblance."

Marshall accompanied his father to the war as a lieutenant, and in a year or two became a captain. In leaving the father here, it may be said that three of his sons were with him in the war, and that he himself served with gallantry and distinction as a colonel. In 1780, he was at the South

with General Lincoln, and being included in
the surrender of that officer and on parole,
visited Kentucky, not yet a State. After a
few years he removed there with the younger
part of his family, leaving Oakhill, as it
seems, in the hands of his son John. He
died in Kentucky in 1806, having survived
to witness the successive honors of his son
culminate in his becoming Chief Justice of
the United States.[1]

[1] It may be added that Thomas Marshall, father of
the Chief Justice, was the son of John Marshall, called
" of the Forest," from the name of his place in Westmoreland County. Of this John it is said, in a little
autobiography of the Chief Justice of some five hundred
words, preserved in Mr. Justice Gray's valuable oration
at Richmond, on February 4, 1901, that his " parents mi-
grated from Wales and settled in the county of Westmoreland in Virginia." The will of " Thomas Marshall,
carpenter," proved May 31, 1704, describing himself as of
Westmoreland County, is printed in the *Virginia Magazine of History*, ii. 343, 344; and it is there stated in
a note that this Thomas "was the first of his race in
America." On the other hand, we are told by an intelligent writer in Appleton's *Cyclopædia of American Biography*, and elsewhere, that the father of " John of the
Forest " was Thomas, born in Virginia in 1655, who died
in 1704; and that it was his father, John, a captain of
cavalry in the service of Charles I., who emigrated to
Virginia about 1650.

It was in the autumn of 1775 that Marshall, as lieutenant in a regiment of minutemen, of which his father was major, marched down through the country to the seaboard to resist Lord Dunmore's aggressions. They were clothed, we are told, in green homespun hunting-shirts, having the words " Liberty or Death " in large letters on the breast, with bucks' tails in their hats, and tomahawks and scalping-knives in their belts. The enemy at Norfolk feared, it is said, for their scalps, but they lost none.[1]

He was thus in the first fighting in Virginia, in the fall of 1775, at Norfolk; afterwards he served in New Jersey, Pennsylvania, and New York; and again in Virginia toward the end of the war. He was at Valley Forge, in the fighting at the Brandywine, Germantown, Monmouth, Stony Point, and Paulus Hook, between 1776 and 1779. He served often as judge advocate, and in this way was brought into personal relations with Washington and Hamilton. A fellow officer and messmate describes him,

[1] Flanders, *Lives of the Chief Justices*, ii. 291.

during the dreadful winter at Valley Forge,
as neither discouraged nor disturbed by anything, content with whatever turned up, and
cheering everybody by his exuberance of
spirits and " his inexhaustible fund of anec-
dote." He was " idolized by the soldiers
and his brother officers."

President Quincy gives us a glimpse of
him at this period, as he heard him described
at a dinner with John Randolph and a large
company of Virginians and other Southern
gentlemen. They were talking of Marshall's
early life and his athletic powers. " It was
said in them that he surpassed any man in
the army; that when the soldiers were idle
at their quarters, it was usual for the officers to engage in matches of quoits, or in
jumping and racing; that he would throw a
quoit farther, and beat at a race any other;
that he was the only man who, with a run-
ning jump, could clear a stick laid on the
heads of two men as tall as himself. On
one occasion he ran in his stocking feet with
a comrade. His mother, in knitting his
stockings, had the legs of blue yarn and the

heels of white. This circumstance, combined with his uniform success in the race, led the soldiers, who were always present at these races, to give him the sobriquet of 'Silver-Heels,' the name by which he was generally known among them."

Toward the end of 1779, owing to the disbanding of Virginia troops at the end of their term of service, he was left without a command, and went to Virginia to await the action of the legislature as to raising new troops. It was a fortunate visit; for at Yorktown he met the young girl who, two or three years later, was to become his wife; and he was also able to improve his leisure by attending, for a few months in the early part of 1780, two courses of lectures at the college, on law and natural philosophy. This was all of college or university that he ever saw; but later, from several of them, he received their highest honors. In 1802 the college of New Jersey (Princeton, where his oldest son, Thomas, was to graduate in 1803), in 1806, Harvard, and in 1815, the University of Pennsylvania, made him

doctor of laws.[1]   Marshall's opportunity for
studying law, under George Wythe, at William
and Mary College, seems to have been
owing to a change in the curriculum, made,
just at that time, at the instance of Jefferson,
governor of the State, and, in that capacity,
visitor of the college.   The chair of
divinity had just been abolished, and one
of law and police, and another of medicine,
were substituted.   On December 29, 1779,
the faculty voted that, " for the encouragement
of science, a student, on paying
annually 1000 pounds of tobacco, shall be
entitled to attend any school of the following
professors, viz. : of Law and Police ; of
Natural Philosophy and Mathematics," etc.
Marshall chose the two courses above named ;
he must have been one of the very first to
avail himself of this new privilege.   He
remained only one term.   In view of what
was to happen by and by, it is interesting to
observe that this opportunity for education
in law came through the agency of Thomas
Jefferson.

[1] His youngest son, Edward Carrington Marshall,
graduated at Harvard in 1826.

The records of the Phi Beta Kappa Society at William and Mary College, where that now famous society had originated less than a year and a half before, show that on the 18th of May, 1780, " Captain John Marshall, being recommended as a gentleman who would make a worthy member of the society, was balloted for and received; " and three days later he was appointed, with others, " to declaim the question whether any form of government is more favorable to public virtue than a Commonwealth." Bushrod Washington and other well-known names are found among his associates in this chapter, which has been well called " an admirable nursery of patriots and statesmen."

It was in the summer of 1780 that Marshall was licensed to practice law.

During this visit to Virginia, as I have said, he met the beautiful little lady, fourteen years old, who became his wife at the age of sixteen, was to be the mother of his ten children,[1] and was to receive from him

[1] Only six of his children grew to full age. See his

the most entire devotion until the day of her
death in 1831. Some letters of her older
sister, Mrs. Carrington, written to another
sister, have lately been printed, which give
us a glimpse of Captain Marshall in his
twenty-fifth year. These ladies were the
daughters of Jaquelin Ambler, formerly col-
lector of customs at Yorktown, and then
treasurer of the colony, and living in that
town, next door to the family of Colonel
Marshall. Their mother was that Rebecca
Burwell, for whom, under the name of " Be-
linda," Jefferson had languished, in his
youthful correspondence of some twenty
years before. The girls had often heard the
captain's letters to his family, and had the
highest expectations when they learned that
he was coming home from the war. They
were to meet him first at a ball, and were
contending for the prize beforehand. Mary,
the youngest, carried it off. " At the first
introduction," writes her sister, who was but

touching letter to Judge Story of June 26, 1831 : " You
ask me if Mrs. Marshall and myself have ever lost a child.
We have lost four," etc. — *Proceedings of the Mass. Hist.
Soc.* (2d series) xiii. 345.

one year older, " he became devoted to her."
" For my own part," she adds, " I felt not the
smallest wish to contest the prize with her.
. . . She, with a glance, divined his character, . . while I, expecting an Adonis, lost
all desire of becoming agreeable in his eyes
when I beheld his awkward, unpolished
manner and total negligence of person."
" How trivial now seem all such objections ! "
she exclaims, writing in 1810, and going on
to speak with the utmost admiration of his
relations to herself and all her family, and
above all, to his wife. " His exemplary tenderness to our unfortunate sister is without
parallel. With a delicacy of frame and
feeling that baffles all description, she became, early after her marriage, a prey to
extreme nervous affection, which, more or
less, has embittered her comfort through
her whole life ; but this has only seemed to
increase his care and tenderness, and he is,
as you know, as entirely devoted as at the
moment of their first being married. Always and under every circumstance an en-
thusiast in love, I have very lately heard

him declare that he looked with astonish-
ment at the present race of lovers, so totally
unlike what he had been himself.  His never-
failing cheerfulness and good humor are a
perpetual source of delight to all connected
with him, and, I have not a doubt, have
been the means of prolonging the life of her
he is so tenderly devoted to."

"He was her devoted lover to the very
end of her life," another member of his family connection has said.  And Judge Story,
in speaking of him after his wife's death,
described him as "the most extraordinary
man I ever saw for the depth and tenderness
of his feelings."

A little touch of his manner to his wife
is seen in a letter, which is in print, written
to her from the city of Washington, on February 23, 1825, in his seventieth year.  He
had received an injury to his knee, about
which Mrs. Marshall was anxious.  "I
shall be out," he writes, "in a few days.
All the ladies of the secretaries have been
to see me, some more than once, and have
brought me more jelly than I could eat, and

many other things. I thank them, and
stick to my barley broth. Still I have lots
of time on my hands. How do you think I
beguile it ? I am almost tempted to leave
you to guess, until I write again. You must
know that I begin with the ball at York,
our splendid assembly at the Palace in Wil-
liamsburg, my visit to Richmond for a fortnight, my return to the field, and the very
welcome reception you gave me on my arrival at Dover, our little tiffs and makings-up,
my feelings when Major Dick [1] was courting
you, my trip to the Cottage [the Ambler
home in Hanover County, where the marriage took place],[2] — the thousand little in-
cidents, deeply affecting, in turn."

This " ball at York " was the one of
which Mrs. Carrington wrote ; and of the
" assembly at the Palace " she also gave an
account, remarking that " Marshall was devoted to my sister."

Miss Martineau, who saw him the year

[1] Richard Anderson, father of Robert Anderson, the
hero of Fort Sumter. See Marion Harland's *Old Colonial Homesteads*, 97.

[2] But see Mrs. Hardy, in *The Green Bag*, viii. 482.

before he died, speaks with great emphasis
of what she calls his " reverence " and his
affectionate respect for women.   There were
many signs of this all through his life.  Even
in the grave and too monotonous course of
his " Life of Washington," one comes now and
then upon a little gleam of this sort, that
lights up the page ; as when he speaks of
Washington's engagement to Mrs. Custis, a
lady " who to a large fortune and a fine person added those amiable accomplishments
which . . . fill with silent but unceasing
felicity the quiet scenes of private life."
When he is returning from France, in 1798,
he writes gayly back from Bordeaux to the
Secretary of Legation at Paris : " Present
me to my friends in Paris ; and have the
goodness to say to Madame Vilette, in my
name and in the handsomest manner, everything which respectful friendship can dic-
tate.   When you have done that, you will
have rendered not quite half justice to my
sentiments."   " He was a man," said Judge
Story, " of deep sensibility and tenderness ;
. . . whatever may be his fame in the eyes

of the world, that which, in a just sense, was his brightest glory was the purity, affectionateness, liberality, and devotedness of his domestic life."

Marshall left the army in 1781, when most of the fighting in Virginia was over; and began practice in Fauquier County when the courts were opened, after Cornwallis's surrender, in October of that year.

Among his neighbors he was always a favorite. In the spring of 1782 he was elected to the Assembly, and in the autumn to the important office of member of the " Privy Council, or Council of State," consisting of eight persons chosen by joint ballot of the two houses of the Assembly. " Young Mr. Marshall," wrote Edmund Pendleton, presiding judge of the Court of Appeals, to Madison, in November of that year, " is elected a councilor. . . . He is clever, but I think too young for that department, which he should rather have earned, as a retirement and reward, by ten or twelve years of hard service." But, whether young or old, the people were for-

ever forcing him into public life. Eight
times he was sent to the Assembly; in 1788
to the Federal Convention of Virginia, and
in 1798 to Congress.

Unwelcome as it was to him, almost always, to have his brilliant and congenial
place and prospects at the bar thus inter-
fered with, we can see now what an admirable preparation all this was for the great
station, which, a little later, to the endless
benefit of his country, he was destined to
fill. What drove him into office so often
was, in a great degree, that delightful and
remarkable combination of qualities which
made everybody love and trust him, even
his political adversaries, so that he could be
chosen when no one else of his party was
available. In this way, happily for his
country, he was led to consider, early and
deeply, those difficult problems of government that distressed the country in the dark
period after the close of the war, and during
the first dozen years of the Federal Constitution.

As regards the effect of his earlier experience in enlarging the circle of a patriot's thoughts and affections, he himself has said: " I am disposed to ascribe my devotion to the Union, and to a government competent to its preservation, at least as much to casual circumstances as to judgment. I had grown up at a time . . . when the maxim, ' United we stand, divided we fall,' was the maxim of every orthodox American; and I had imbibed these sentiments so thoroughly that they constituted a part of my being. I carried them with me into the army, where I found myself associated with brave men from different States who were risking life and everything valuable in a common cause ; . . . and where I was confirmed in the habit of considering America as my country and Congress as my government." It was this confirmed " habit of considering America as my country," communicated by him to his countrymen, which enabled them to carry through the great struggle of forty years ago, and to save for us all, North and South, the inestimable treasure of the Union.

After Marshall's marriage, in January,

1783, he made Richmond his home for the rest of his life. It was still a little town, but it had lately become the capital of the State, and the strongest men at the bar gradually gathered there. Marshall met them all. One has only to look at the law reports of Call and Washington to see the place that he won. He is found in most of the important cases. In his time no man's name occurs oftener, probably none so often.

The earliest case in which the printed reports show his name is that of Hite *v.* Fairfax (4 Call's Reports, 42), in May, 1786, and his argument seems to be fully reported. It was a very important case, and Marshall represented tenants of Lord Fairfax. There were conflicting grants on the famous "Northern Neck" of Virginia, an extensive region given by the crown to Lord Fairfax's ancestor, whose boundaries had been in dispute. It comprised the land between the Potomac and the Rappahannock, "within the heads of the rivers . . . the courses of the said rivers, as they are commonly called or known by the inhabitants and descriptions of those parts, and Chesapeake Bay, together with the rivers themselves and all the islands within the banks of the rivers." This description was finally admitted by the crown (in 1745) to include all the land between the head springs of the Potomac and those of the south branch of the Rappahannock. Bishop Meade[1] describes it as the region which, beginning on the Chesapeake Bay, lies between the Potomac and Rappahannock rivers, and crossing the Blue Ridge, or passing through it with the Potomac at Harper's Ferry, extends with that river to the heads thereof in the Alleghany Mountains, and thence by a straight line crosses the North Mountain and Blue Ridge at the headwaters of the Rappahannock, . . . the most fertile part of Virginia."

Marshall had now to meet a total denial of Lord Fairfax's title. His argument of ten or twelve pages shows already the characteristics, the cogency, clear method, and neat precision of thought and speech, by which his later work was marked. " I had

[1] *Old Churches and Families of Virginia*, ii. 105.

conceived," he says, " that it was not more
certain that there was such a tract of
country as the Northern Neck than that
Lord Fairfax was the proprietor of it. . . .
Gentlemen cannot suppose that a grant
made by the crown to the ancestor for services rendered or even for affection can be
invalidated in the hands of an heir because
these services and affections are forgotten,
or because the thing granted has, from causes
which must have been foreseen, become
more valuable than when it was given. And
if it could not be invalidated in the hands
of the heir, much less can it be in the hands
of the purchaser." As regards the construction of the grant: " Whether Lord
Fairfax's grant extended originally beyond
the forks of the rivers or not, will no more
admit of argument than it ever could have
admitted of a doubt. But whether it should
be bounded by the north or south fork of the
Rappahannock was a question involved in
more uncertainty. . . . It is, however, no
longer a question, for it has been decided.
. . . That decision did not create or extend

Lord Fairfax's right, but determined what the right originally was. The bounds of many patents are doubtful; the extent of many titles uncertain : but when a decision is once made on them, it removes the doubt and ascertains what the original boundaries were." In reference to a personal appeal in behalf of certain settlers, he says, " Those who explore and settle new countries are generally bold, hardy, and adventurous men, whose minds as well as bodies are fitted to encounter danger and fatigue ; their object is the acquisition of property, and they generally succeed. None will say that the complainants have failed ; and if their hardships and dangers have any weight in the court, the defendants share in them, and have equal claim to countenance ; for they, too, with humbler views and less extensive prospects, have explored, bled for, and settled a till then uncultivated desert."

Compare with this the like simple felicity and exactness of expression in his last reported utterance in court, when he was closing his great career as Chief Justice of the

United States, forty-nine years later.   He is
refusing a motion for delay: " The court has
taken into its serious and anxious consideration the motion made on the part of the
government to continue the cause of Mitchel
v. The United States to the next term.
Though the hope of deciding causes to the
mutual satisfaction of parties would be
chimerical, that of convincing them that
the case has been fully and fairly considered, that due attention has been given
to the arguments of counsel, and that the
best judgment of the court has been exercised on the case, may be sometimes indulged.   Even this is not always attainable.
In the excitement produced by ardent controversy, gentlemen view the same object
through such different media that minds
not unfrequently receive therefrom precisely opposite impressions.   The court, however, must see with its own eyes, and exercise its own judgment guided by its own
reason. . . . The opinion of the court will
be delivered." [1]

[1] It was given by another judge.

At first, he had brought from the army, and from his home on the frontier, simple and rustic ways which surprised some persons at Richmond, whose conception of greatness was associated with very different models of dress and behavior. "He was one morning strolling," we are told, "through the streets of Richmond, attired in a plain linen roundabout and shorts, with his hat under his arm, from which he was eating cherries, when he stopped in the porch of the Eagle Hotel, indulged in a little pleasantry with the landlord, and then passed on." A gentleman from the country was present, who had a case coming on before the Court of Appeals, and was referred by the landlord to Marshall as the best lawyer to employ. But "the careless, languid air" of Marshall had so prejudiced the man that he refused to employ him. The clerk, when this client entered the court-room, also recommended Marshall, but the other would have none of him. A venerable-looking lawyer, with powdered wig and in black cloth, soon entered, and the gentleman en-

gaged him. In the first case that came up,
this man and Marshall spoke on opposite
sides. The gentleman listened, saw his mistake, and secured Marshall at once; frankly
telling him the whole story, and adding that
while he had come with one hundred dollars
to pay his lawyer, he had but five dollars
left. Marshall good-naturedly took this, and
helped in the case. In the Virginia Federal
Convention of 1788, at the age of thirty-
three, he is described, rising after Monroe
had spoken, as "a tall young man, slovenly
dressed in loose summer apparel. . . . His
manners, like those of Monroe, were in
strange contrast with those of Edmund Randolph or of Grayson."

In such stories as these, one is reminded,
as he is often reminded, of a resemblance
between Marshall and Lincoln. Very different men they were, but both thorough
Americans, with unborrowed character and
manners, and a lifelong flavor derived from
no other soil.

At the height of Marshall's reputation, in
1797, a French writer, who had visited Rich-

mond lately, in speaking of Edmund Randolph, says, " He has a great practice, and stands, in that respect, nearly on a par with Mr. J. Marshall, the most esteemed and celebrated counselor of this town." He mentions Marshall's annual income as being four or five thousand dollars. " Even by his friends," it is added, " he is taxed with some little propensity to indolence, but he nevertheless displays great superiority when he applies his mind to business." Another contemporary, who praises his force and eloquence in speaking, yet says : " It is difficult to rouse his faculties. He begins with reluctance, hesitation, and vacancy of eye. . . . He reminds one of some great bird, which flounders on the earth for a while before it acquires impetus to sustain its soaring flight." And finally, William Wirt, who was seventeen years Marshall's junior, and came to the bar in 1792, when Marshall was nearly at the head of it, writing anonymously in 1804, describes him as one, " who, without the advantage of person, voice, attitude, gesture, or any of the ornaments of an

orator, deserves to be considered as one of
the most eloquent men in the world." He
attributes to him " one original and almost
supernatural faculty, . . . of developing a
subject by a single glance of his mind. . . .
His eyes do not fly over a landscape and
take in its various objects with more prompt-
itude and facility than his mind embraces
and analyzes the most complex subject. . . .
All his eloquence consists in the apparently
deep self-conviction and the emphatic earnestness and energy of his style, the close and
logical connection of his thoughts, and the
easy gradations by which he opens his lights
on the attentive minds of his hearers."

In 1789 he declined the office of District
Attorney of the United States at Richmond,[1]
in 1795 that of Attorney-General of the
United States, and in 1796 that of Minister
to France, all offered him by Washington.
When President Adams persuaded him, in
1797, to go, with Pinckney and Gerry, as

[1] Mr. Justice Gray preserves this fact in his address on
Marshall.   His commission bore the same date with that
of Chief Justice Jay, September 26, 1789, — two days after
the approval of the Judiciary Act.

envoy to France, he wrote to Gerry of
" General Marshall " (as he was then called,
from his rank of brigadier general, since
1793, in the Virginia militia), " He is a
plain man, very sensible, cautious, guarded,
and learned in the law of nations." The
extraordinary details of that unsuccessful
six months' attempt to come to terms with
France are found in Marshall's very able
dispatches and in the diary which he kept; [1]
for, with the instinct of a man of affairs, he
failed not to remember, with Thomas Gray,
that " a note is worth a cartload of recollec-
tions." His own part in the business was
marked by great moderation and ability;
and on his return, in 1798, he was received
at Philadelphia with remarkable demonstra-
tions and the utmost enthusiasm. A corre-
spondent of Rufus King, writing from New
York in July of that year, says, " No two
men can be more beloved and honored than
Pinckney and Marshall;" and again in November: " Saving General Washington, I
believe the President, Pinckney, and Mar-

[1] See Wait's *State Papers*, iii. 165–304.

shall are the most popular characters now in
our country.   There is a certain something
in the correspondence of Pinckney and Marshall . . . that has united all heads and
hearts in their eulogy." It is understood
that the American side of this correspondence was by Marshall.   Gerry had allowed
himself in a measure to be detached by the
Directory from his associates, to their great
displeasure.   With them, in important respects, he disagreed.

Among those who paid their respects to
Marshall, on his return from France, was
Thomas Jefferson, the Vice-President, whose
correspondence shows him at the time expressing the most unflattering opinion of the
envoys.   Jefferson wrote to Marshall the following note : " In after years," says Mrs.
Hardy, one of Marshall's descendants,[1] "the
Chief Justice frequently laughed over it,
saying, ' Mr. Jefferson came very near telling me the truth ; the added *un* to *lucky*,
policy alone demanded.' " The note ran
thus : " Thos. Jefferson presents his compli-

[1] *The Green Bag*, viii. 482.

ments to General Marshall. He had the
honor of calling at his lodgings twice this
morning, but was so ~unlucky~ as to find that
he was out on both occasions. He wished to
have expressed in person his regret that a
pre-engagement for to-day, which could not
be dispensed with, would prevent him the
satisfaction of dining in company with Genl-
Marshall, and, therefore, begs leave to place
here the expressions of that respect which in
company with his fellow-citizens he bears him.

" Genl. Marshall,
        at Oeller's Hotel, June 23d, 1798."

In 1798 Adams offered to Marshall the
seat on the Supreme Bench, made vacant by
the death of James Wilson. He declined
it ; and it went to his old associate at William and Mary College, Bushrod Washington. Marshall did yield, however, to General
Washington's urgent request to stand for
Congress that year. He held out long
against Washington's arguments, and only
yielded, at last, when that venerated man
called attention to his own recent sacrifice
in accepting the unwelcome place of lieu-

tenant-general of the army. When that
went into the scale it was too much. Marshall was then on a visit to Mount Vernon,
whither he had been invited in August or
September, in company with Washington's
nephew, the coming judge.

On their way to Mount Vernon, the two
travelers met with a misadventure which
gave great amusement to Washington, and
of which he enjoyed telling his friends.
They came on horseback, and carried but
one pair of saddlebags, each using one side.
Arriving thoroughly drenched by rain, they
were shown to a chamber to change their
garments. One opened his side of the bags
and drew forth a black bottle of whiskey.
He insisted that he had opened his companion's repository. Unlocking the other side,
they found a big twist of tobacco, some corn
bread, and the equipment of a pack-saddle.
They had exchanged saddlebags with some
traveler, and now had to appear in a ludicrous misfit of borrowed clothes.[1]

[1] Paulding's *Life of Washington*, ii. 191; *Lippincott's
Magazine*, ii. 624, 625.

The election of Marshall to Congress ex-
cited great interest.[1]  Washington heartily
rejoiced in it.  Jefferson, on the other hand,
remarked that while Marshall might trouble
the Republicans somewhat, yet he would now
be unmasked.  He had been popular with
the mass of the people, Jefferson said, from
his " lax, lounging manners," and with wiser
men through a " profound hypocrisy."  But
now his British principles would stand revealed.

The New England Federalists were very
curious about him ; they had been alarmed
and outraged, during the campaign, by his
expressing opposition to the alien and sedition laws ; but they were much impressed
by him.  Theodore Sedgwick wrote to Rufus

---

[1] In an amusing account of this election (Munford's
*The Two Parsons*), we are told that the sheriff presided,
with the two candidates, Marshall and John Clopton,
seated on the justice's bench.  The voter, being asked
for whom he voted, gave the name of his candidate ; and
the latter thanked him ; *e. g.*, " Your vote is appreciated,
sir," said Marshall to his friend Parson Blair.  For an
account of the same method of conducting elections in
Virginia at a later period, see John S. Wise's *The End
of an Era.*

King that he had "great powers, and much
dexterity in the application of them. . . .
We can do nothing without him." But
Sedgwick wished that "his education had
been on the other side of the Delaware."
George Cabot wrote to King: "General
Marshall is a leader. . . . But you see in
him the faults of a Virginian. . . . He thinks
too much of that State, and he expects that
the world will be governed by rules of logic."
But Cabot hopes to see him improve, and
adds, "He seems calculated to act a great
part." In the end, the Northern Federalists
were disappointed in finding him too mod-
erate. He held the place of leader of the
House, and passed into the cabinet in May,
1800. On January 31, 1801, he was commissioned as Chief Justice.

## CHAPTER II

THERE is little room for quotations from Marshall's speeches or dispatches.

Some reference has already been made to his earliest reported argument in court, in 1786. In the Virginia Federal Convention, in 1788, Marshall's principal speeches related to the subjects of taxation, the militia, and the judiciary. These, so far as preserved, are found in the third volume of Elliot's Debates, and in Dr. Grigsby's very interesting History of that Convention, in the tenth volume of the " Virginia Historical Collections." Nothing remains of a famous speech in support of Jay's treaty, at a public meeting in Richmond in 1795. A summary of his strong but unsuccessful argument in 1796, in the case of Ware v. Hylton (3 Dallas 199), as to the claims of British

creditors, his only case before the Supreme
Court of the United States, is preserved in
the volume of reports. This argument attracted much attention among the statesmen
at Philadelphia. "I then became acquainted,"
he wrote to a friend, "with Mr. Cabot, Mr.
Ames, Mr. Dexter, and Mr. Sedgwick of
Massachusetts, Mr. Wadsworth of Connecticut, and Mr. King of New York. . . .
I was particularly intimate with Mr. Ames."

After Washington's death in 1799, Marshall, in a short and well-known speech,
moved the resolution of the House of Representatives.

A little afterwards he made a great and
admirably thorough address in a matter which
then deeply affected the public mind; from
this, his greatest public speech,[1] a quotation
is given below. It was made March 4, 1800,

[1] "The masterly and conclusive argument of John
Marshall in the House of Representatives. 8 Stat. 129;
Wharton's State Trials, 392; Bee [Reports], 286; 5 Wheat.
appendix 3." — Gray, J., speaking for the Supreme Court
of the United States, in Fong Yue Ting *v.* U. S., 149 U. S.
698, 714. This speech is also found in Moore's *American
Eloquence*, ii. 7.

in defense of the President's action in the case of Thomas Nash, *alias* Jonathan Robbins. This person, a British subject, but claiming to be an American citizen, and to have been impressed into the British navy, was charged with piracy and murder on board a British ship of war in 1791. Being found in Charleston, S. C., he was arrested in 1799, at the instance of the British consul, and held to await an application for his extradition under article 27 of the treaty with Great Britain of 1795. That article bound the two countries reciprocally to deliver up, on request of the other, persons charged with murder committed within the jurisdiction of that other. Evidence of criminality was first to be furnished, such as would justify commitment for trial on the same charge in the country where the accused was found.

An application for extradition was made to the federal authorities in Charleston, but at their suggestion this was transferred to the President, through the Secretary of State. The Secretary informed Bee, the

United States District Judge, of the President's " advice and request " that Nash should be delivered up, at the same time referring to the clause in the treaty as to the necessary evidence of criminality.[1] The judge on July 1, 1799, informed the Secretary that he had notified the British consul that on the production of such evidence, the prisoner would be delivered up when the consul was ready to receive him. The delivery was made ; and on September 9 of the same year, the British admiral was able to inform the British Minister that Nash " has been tried at a court martial, and sentenced to suffer death, and afterwards hung in chains ; which sentence has been put into execution."

These events were used with great effect by the political opponents of the administration. When Congress met, the President was called upon by the House of Repre-

[1] The President had written to the Secretary of State from Quincy, May 21, 1799 : " How far the President of the United States would be justified in directing the judge to deliver up the offender is not clear. I have no objection to advise, and request him to do so." Wharton's State Trials, 418.

sentatives for the papers relating to them;
and when they were sent in, Edward Livingston, of New York, submitted resolutions
condemning the action of the executive, on
the ground that the determination of the
questions involved in the case " are all matters exclusively for judicial inquiry;" that
the acts of the President " are a dangerous
interference of the executive with judicial
decisions;" and that the compliance of the
district judge " is a sacrifice of the constitutional independence of the judicial power."
After a full debate, these resolutions were
negatived by a decided vote.    Marshall's
very able argument vindicated the action
taken, and laid down principles which have
ever since governed the course of the government in such cases.

The following passages will afford a speci-
men of the style and method of this address,
a style and method which were characteristic
of all Marshall's work: —

" The same argument applies to the observations on the seventh article of the
amendment to the Constitution.    That arti-

cle relates only to trials in the courts of the
United States, and not to the performance
of a contract for the delivery of a murderer
not triable in those courts.

" In this part of the argument, the gentleman from New York [Mr. Livingston] has
presented a dilemma, of a very wonderful
structure indeed.   He says that the offense
of Thomas Nash was either a crime or not a
crime.   If it was a crime, the constitutional
mode of punishment ought to have been
observed; if it was not a crime, he ought
not to have been delivered up to a foreign
government, where his punishment was inevitable.

" It has escaped the observation of that
gentleman that if the murder committed by
Thomas Nash was a crime, yet it was not a
crime provided for by the Constitution or
triable in the courts of the United States;
and that if it was not a crime, yet it is the
precise case in which his surrender was stipulated by treaty.   Of this extraordinary
dilemma, the gentleman from New York is
himself perfectly at liberty to retain either
form.

" He has chosen to consider it as a crime, and says it has been made a crime by treaty, and is punished by sending the offender out of the country. The gentleman is incorrect in every part of his statement. Murder on board a British frigate is not a crime created by treaty. It would have been a crime of precisely the same magnitude had the treaty never been formed. It is not punished by sending the offender out of the United States. The experience of the unfortunate criminal, who was hung and gibbeted, evinced to him that the punishment of his crime was of a much more serious nature than mere banishment from the United States.

" The gentleman from Pennsylvania [Mr. Gallatin] and the gentleman from Virginia [Mr. Nicholas] have both contended that this was a case proper for the decision of the courts, because points of law occurred, and points of law must have been decided in its determination. The points of law which must have been decided are stated by the gentleman from Pennsylvania to be, first, a question whether the offense was committed within the British jurisdiction; and, secondly, whether the crime charged was comprehended within the treaty.

" It is true, sir, these points of law must have occurred, and must have been decided, but it by no means follows that they could only have been decided in court. A variety of legal questions must present themselves in the performance of every executive duty, but these questions are not therefore to be decided in court. Whether a patent for land shall issue or not is always a question of law, but not a question which must necessarily be carried into court. The gentleman from Pennsylvania seems to have permitted himself to have been misled by the misrepresentations of the Constitution made in the resolutions of the gentleman from New York; and, in consequence of being so misled, his observations have the appearance of endeavoring to fit the Constitution to his arguments, instead of adapting his arguments to the Constitution.

" When the gentleman has proved that these are questions of law, and that they must have been decided by the President, he has not advanced a single step towards proving that they were improper for executive decision.    The question whether vessels captured within three miles of the American coast, or by privateers fitted out in the American ports, were legally captured or not, and whether the American government is bound to restore them, if in its power, were questions of law, but they were questions of political law, proper to be decided, and they were decided by the executive, and not by the courts.    The *casus fœderis* of the guaranty was a question of law, but no man could have hazarded the opinion that such a question must be carried into court, and can only be there decided.    So the *casus fœderis*, under the twenty-seventh article of the treaty with Britain, is a question of law, but of political law.    The question to be decided is, whether the particular case proposed be one in which the nation has bound itself to act, and this is a question depending on principles never submitted to courts.    If murder should be committed

within the United States, and the murderer
should seek an asylum in Britain, the question whether the *casus fœderis*, of the
twenty-seventh article had occurred, so that
his delivery ought to be demanded, would
be a question of law, but no man would say
it was a question which ought to be decided
in the courts.

" When, therefore, the gentleman from
Pennsylvania has established that, in deliver-
ing up Thomas Nash, points of law were
decided by the President, he has established
a position which in no degree whatever aids
his argument. The case is in its nature a
national demand, made upon the nation.
The parties are the two nations.  They cannot come into court to litigate their claims,
nor can a court decide on them.  Of consequence, the demand is not a case for judicial
cognizance.  The President is the sole organ
of the nation in its external relations, and
its sole representative with foreign nations.
Of consequence, the demand of a foreign
nation can only be made on him. . . .

" The treaty, which is a law, enjoins the

performance of a particular object. The person who is to perform this object is marked out by the Constitution, since the person is named who conducts the foreign intercourse and is to take care that the laws be faithfully executed. The means by which it is to be performed, the force of the nation, are in the hands of this person. Ought not this person to perform the object, although the particular mode of using the means has not been prescribed? Congress, unquestionably, may prescribe the mode, and Congress may devolve on others the whole execution of the contract; but, till this is done, it seems the duty of the executive department to execute the contract by any means it possesses.

"The gentleman from Pennsylvania contends that, although this should be properly an executive duty, yet it cannot be performed until Congress shall direct the mode of performance. . . . The treaty stipulating that a murderer shall be delivered up to justice is as obligatory as an act of Congress making the same declaration. If, then,

there was an act of Congress in the words
of the treaty, declaring that a person who
had committed murder within the jurisdiction of Britain, and sought an asylum within
the territory of the United States, should be
delivered up by the United States, on the
demand of his Britannic Majesty and such
evidence of his criminality as would have
justified his commitment for trial, had the
offense been committed here; could the
President, who is bound to execute the laws,
have justified the refusal to deliver up the
criminal by saying that the legislature had
totally omitted to provide for the case?

" The executive is not only the constitutional department, but seems to be the
proper department to which the power in
question may most wisely and most safely be
confided. . . . If, at any time, policy may
temper the strict execution of the contract,
where may that political discretion be placed
so safely as in the department whose duty it
is to understand precisely the state of the
political intercourse and connection between
the United States and foreign nations, to

understand the manner in which the particular stipulation is explained and performed
by foreign nations, and to understand com-
pletely the state of the Union?"

This clear, strong, convincing speech, of
which I have quoted but a small portion,
settled the question then in dispute, and the
principles here laid down have controlled
the action of the government ever since.

Very soon after entering upon his duties
as Chief Justice, Marshall undertook to write
the " Life of Washington." This gave him a
great deal of trouble and mortification.    It
proved to be an immense labor ; the pub-
lishers were importunate, and he was driven
into print before he was ready.    The result
was a work in five volumes, appearing from
1802 to 1804, full of the most valuable and
authentic material, well repaying perusal,
yet put together with singular lack of liter-
ary skill, and in many ways a great disappointment.[1]    In the later years of his life,

[1] The short " autobiography " before referred to (*ante*,
p. 10, n.) ends thus: " I have written no book except

he revised it, corrected some errors, short-
ened it, and published it in three volumes:
one of them, in 1824, as a separate preliminary history of the colonial period, and the
other two, in 1834, as the " Life of Washington." This work, in its original form, gave
great offense to Jefferson, written, as it was,
from the point of view of a constant admirer
and supporter of the policy of Washington;
a " five volume libel," Jefferson called it.

Jefferson had ludicrous misconceptions as
to Marshall's real character. It is said that
after Burr's trial, in 1807, all personal intercourse between them ceased.[1] Referring
in 1810 to the " batture " case, in which
Edward Livingston sued him, and which
was to come before Marshall, Jefferson says
that he is certain what the result of the
case should be, but nobody can tell what it
will be; for " the Judge's mind [is] of that
gloomy malignity which will never let him
forego the opportunity of satiating it upon a

the ' Life of Washington,' which was executed with so
much precipitation as to require much correction."
[1] Van Santvoord, *Lives of the Chief Justices*, 343, n.

victim. . . . And to whom is my appeal?
From the judge in Burr's case to himself
and his associate justices in Marbury *v.*
Madison. Not exactly, however. I observe
old Cushing is dead. [Judge Cushing had
died a fortnight before.] At length, then,
we have a chance of getting a Republican
majority in the Supreme Judiciary." And
he goes on to express his confidence in the
" appointment of a decided Republican, with
nothing equivocal about him."

Who was this decided and unequivocal
Republican to be? Jefferson was anxious
about it, and wrote to Madison, suggesting
Judge Tyler, of Virginia, as a candidate,
and reminding the President of Marshall's
" rancorous hostility to his country." Who
was it, in fact, that was appointed? Who
but Joseph Story! — a Republican, indeed,
but one whom Jefferson, in this very year,
was designating as a " pseudo-Republican,"
and who soon became Marshall's warmest
admirer and most faithful supporter.

## CHAPTER III

THE BEGINNINGS OF THE CHIEF JUSTICE'S
CAREER ; AMERICAN CONSTITUTIONAL
LAW ; MARBURY *v.* MADISON.

MARSHALL'S accession to the bench was
marked by an impressive circumstance. For
ten years or more, he alone gave all the
opinions of the court to which any name
was attached, except where the case came up
from his own circuit, or, for any reason, he
did not sit. In the very few cases where
opinions were given by the other justices, it
was in the old way, *seriatim*, — the method
followed before Marshall came in, as it was
also the method of contemporary English
courts.

Whatever may have been the purpose of
the Chief Justice in introducing this usage,
there can be no doubt as to the impression
it was calculated to produce. It seemed, all
of a sudden, to give to the judicial depart-

ment a unity like that of the executive, to concentrate the whole force of that department in its chief, and to reduce the side-justices to a sort of cabinet advisers. In the very few early cases where there was expressed dissent, it lost much of its impressiveness, when announced, as it sometimes was, by the mouth that gave the opinion of the court.

In 1812, when a change took place, the court had been for a year without a quorum. Moreover, Judge Story had just come to the bench, a man of quite too exuberant an intellect and temperament to work well as a silent side-judge. We remark, also, at the beginning of that term, that the Chief Justice was not in attendance, having, as the reporter tells us, " received an injury by the oversetting of the stage-coach on his journey from Richmond." And it may be added that just at this time the anxious prayer of Jefferson was answered, and a majority of the judges were Republicans. From whatever cause, henceforward there was a change ; and without returning to the old

habit of *seriatim* opinions, the side-judges
had their turn, as they do now.

In most of Marshall's opinions, one ob-
serves the style and special touch of a
thoughtful and original mind ; in some of
them the powers of a great mind, in full activity. His cases relating to international
law, as I am assured by those competent to
judge, rank with the best there are in the
books. As regards most of the more familiar titles of the law, it would be too much
to claim for him the very first rank. In
that region he is, in many respects, equaled
or surpassed by men more deeply versed in
the learning and technicalities of the law, in
what constitutes that " artificial perfection
of reason " which Coke used to glorify as
far transcending any man's natural reason,
— men such as Story, Kent, or Shaw, or
even the reformer, Mansfield, whom he
greatly admired, Eldon, or Blackburn. But
in the field of constitutional law, a region
not open to an English lawyer, — and especially in one department of it, that relating to the nature and scope of the National

Constitution, he was preëminent, — first, with no one second. It is hardly possible, as regards this part of the law, to say too much of the service he rendered to his country. Sitting in the highest judicial place for more than a generation; familiar, from the beginning, with the Federal Constitution, with the purposes of its framers, and with all the objections of its critics; accustomed to meet these objections from the time he had served in the Virginia Convention of 1788; convinced of the purpose and capacity of this instrument to create a strong nation, competent to make itself respected at home and abroad, and able to speak with the voice and strike with the strength of all; assured that this was the paramount necessity of the country, and that the great source of danger was in the jealousies and adverse interests of the States, — Marshall acted on his convictions. He determined to give full effect to all the affirmative contributions of power that went to make up a great and efficient national government; and fully, also, to enforce the national re-

straints and prohibitions upon the States.
In both cases he included not only the powers
expressed in the Constitution, but those also
which should be found, as time unfolded, to
be fairly and clearly implied in the objects
for which the federal government was established.    In that long judicial life, with which
Providence blessed him, and blessed his
country, he was able to lay down, in a succession of cases, the fundamental considerations which fix and govern the relative functions of the nation and the States, so plainly,
with such fullness, with such simplicity and
strength of argument, such a candid allowance for all that was to be said upon the
other side, in a tone so removed from con-
troversial bitterness, so natural and fit for a
great man addressing the " serene reason "
of mankind, as to commend these things to
the minds of his countrymen, and firmly to
fix them in the jurisprudence of the nation ;
so that " when the rain descended and the
floods came, and the winds blew and beat
upon that house, it fell not, because it was
founded upon a rock."    It was Marshall's

strong constitutional doctrine, explained in
detail, elaborated, powerfully argued, over
and over again, with unsurpassable earnestness and force, placed permanently in our
judicial records, holding its own during the
long emergence of a feebler political theory,
and showing itself in all its majesty when
war and civil dissension came, — it was
largely this that saved the country from suc-
cumbing, in the great struggle of forty years
ago, and kept our political fabric from going
to pieces.

I do not forget our own Webster, or
others, in saying that to Marshall (if we
may use his own phrase about Washington), "more than to any other individual,
and as much as to one individual was possible," do we owe that prevalence of sound
constitutional opinion and doctrine at the
North that held the Union together; to that
combination in him, of a great statesman's
sagacity, a great lawyer's lucid exposition
and persuasive reasoning, a great man's can-
dor and breadth of view, and that judicial
authority on the bench, allowed naturally

and as of right, to a large, sweet nature,
which all men loved and trusted, capable of
harmonizing differences and securing the
largest possible amount of coöperation among
discordant associates.  In a very great degree, it was Marshall, and these things in
him, that have wrought out for us a strong
and great nation, one which men can love
and die for ; that "mother of a mighty race,"
that stirred the soul of Bryant half a century
ago, as he dreamed how —

> " The thronging years in glory rise,
>        And as they fleet,
>     Drop strength and riches at thy feet ; "

the nation whose image flamed in the heart
of Lowell, a generation since, as he greeted
her coming up out of the Valley of the
Shadow of Death : —

> " Oh Beautiful, my country, ours once more ! . . .
> Among the nations bright beyond compare ! . . .
> What were our lives without thee ?
> What all our lives to save thee ?
> We reck not what we gave thee,
> We will not dare to doubt thee,
> But ask whatever else, and we will dare ! "

It was early in Marshall's day that the
Supreme Court first took the grave step of
disregarding an act of Congress, — a coördinate department, — which conflicted with the
National Constitution.  The right to deal
thus with their legislatures had already been
asserted in the States, and once or twice it
had really been exercised.  Had the question related to a conflict between that Constitution and the enactment of a State, it
would have been a simpler matter.  These
two questions, under European written constitutions, are regarded as different ones.  It
is almost necessary to the working of a federal system that the general government, and
each of its departments, should be free to
disregard acts of any department of the local
states which may be inconsistent with the
federal constitution.  And so in Switzerland
and Germany the federal courts thus treat
local enactments.  But there is not under
any written constitution in Europe a country
where a court deals in this way with the
act of its coördinate legislature.  In Germany, at one time, this was done, under the

influence of a study of our law, but it was
soon abandoned.[1]

In the colonial period, while we were de-
pendencies of Great Britain, our legislation
was subject to the terms of the royal charters.    Enactments were often disallowed by
the English Privy Council, sometimes acting
as mere revisers of the colonial legislation,
and sometimes as appellate judicial tribu-
nals.    Our people were, in this way, familiar
with the theory of a dependent legislature,
one whose action was subject to reversal by
judicial authority, as contrary to the terms
of a written charter of government.

When, therefore, after the war of independence, our new sovereign, namely, our-
selves, the people, came to substitute for the
old royal charters the people's charters, what
we call our " constitutions," — it was natural
to expect some legal restraint upon legislation.    It was not always found in terms;
indeed, it was at first hardly ever, if at all,
found set down in words.    But it was a

---

[1] Coxe, *Jud. Power*, 95–102 ; Thayer's *Cases on Constitutional Law*, i. 146–149.

natural and just interpretation of these in-
struments, made in regions with such a history as ours and growing out of the midst of
such ideas and such an experience, to think
that courts, in the regular exercise of their
functions, that is to say, in dealing with litigated cases, could treat the constitutions as
law to be applied by them in determining
the validity of legislation.

But this, although, as we may well think,
a sound conclusion, was not a necessary one ;
and it was long denied by able statesmen,
judges, and lawyers. An elaborate and
powerful dissenting opinion by Chief Justice
Gibson, of Pennsylvania, containing the most
searching argument on the subject with
which I am acquainted, given in 1825,[1]
reaches the result that under no constitution where the power to set aside legislative
enactments is not expressly given, does it
exist. But it is recognized that in the Federal Constitution the power is given, as regards legislation of the States inconsistent
with the Federal Constitution and laws.

[1] Eakin v. Raub, 12 Sergeant & Rawle, 330.

It is not always noticed that in making our
Federal Constitution, there was an avoidance
of any explicit declaration of such a power
as touching federal legislation, while it was
carefully provided for as regards the States.
In the Federal Convention, there was great
anxiety to control the States, in certain par-
ticulars; and various plans were put forward, such as that Congress should have a
negative on state laws, and that governors
of the States should be appointed by the
federal authority, with power to negative
state acts.

But all these, at last, were rejected, and
the matter took the shape of a provision that
the Constitution and the constitutional laws
and treaties of the United States should be
the supreme law of *the respective States;*
and the judges of *the several States* should
be bound thereby, anything in the constitution or laws of any State to the contrary
notwithstanding.   Later, the Committee on
Style changed the phrase "law of the respective States" to "law of the land."   But
the language, as to binding the judges, was

still limited to the judges of the several States. Observe, then, the scope of this provision : it was to secure the authority of the federal system within the States.

As to any method of protecting the federal system within its own household, that is to say, as against Congress, it was proposed in the convention, for one thing, that each House of Congress might call upon the judges for opinions ; and, again, it was urged, and that repeatedly and with great persistence, that the judges should be joined with the executive in passing on the approval or disapproval of legislative acts, — in what we call the veto power. It was explicitly said, in objecting to this, that the judges would have the right to disregard unconstitutional laws anyway, — an opinion put forward by some of the weightiest members. Yet some denied it. And we observe that the power was not expressly given. When we find such a power expressly denied, and yet not expressly given ; and when we observe, for example, that leading public men, e. g., so conspicuous a member of the con-

vention as Charles Pinckney of South Carolina, afterwards a senator from that State,
wholly denied the power ten years later;[1] it
being also true that he and others of his way
of thinking urged the express restraints on
state legislation, — we may justly reach the
conclusion that this question, while not over-
looked, was intentionally left untouched.
Like the question of the bank and various
others, presumably it was so left in order
not to stir up enemies to the new instrument; left to be settled by the silent determinations of time, or by later discussion.

Turning now to the actual practice under
the government of the United States, we find
that the judges of the Supreme Court had
hardly taken their seats, at the beginning of

[1] What Pinckney said in 1799 was this: "Upon no
subject am I more convinced than that it is an unsafe
and dangerous doctrine in a republic ever to suppose that
a judge ought to possess the right of questioning or deciding upon the constitutionality of treaties, laws, or any
act of the legislature. It is placing the opinion of an
individual, or of two or three, above that of both branches
of Congress, a doctrine which is not warranted by the
Constitution, and will not, I hope, long have many advo-
cates in this country." Wharton, *State Trials*, 412.

the government, when Chief Justice Jay and
several other judges, in 1790, communicated
to the President objections to the Judiciary
Act, as violating the Constitution, in naming
the judges of the Supreme Court to be judges
also of the circuit courts.[1]   These judges,
however, did not refuse to act under this unconstitutional statute; and the question did
not come judicially before the court until
Marshall's time, in 1803,[2] when it was held
that the question must now be regarded as
settled in favor of the statute, by reason of
acquiescence since the beginning of the government.[3]

[1] 4 Amer. Jurist, 293 ; Story, Const. § 1579, n.

[2] Stuart v. Laird, 1 Cranch, 299.

[3] Marshall, when the act of 1802 restored the old system, stated to his associates his deliberate agreement
with the opinion expressed by his predecessors above
referred to, and proposed to refuse to sit in the circuit
court.   All his brethren agreed with his view on the constitutional point, but thought the question should be regarded as at rest, by reason of the earlier practice of the
court, up to 1801.   This view prevailed, and was soon
afterwards, as above stated, judicially adopted by the
court.   This statement is made by Chancellor Kent in
3 N. Y. Review, 347 (1838).

For the knowledge of the authorship of this valuable
article and of another related one in 2 ib. 372, I am in-

In observing, historically, the earlier conceptions of the judges of the Supreme Court as to the method of dealing with unconstitutional legislation, one or two other transactions should be looked at. In 1792 (1 U. S. Statutes, 243) a statute was enacted which required the circuit court, partly composed, as we have seen, of the judges of the Supreme Court, to pass on the claims of certain soldiers and others demanding pensions, and to report to the Secretary of War; who was, in turn, to revise these returns and report to Congress. The judges found great difficulty in acting under this statute, because it imposed on them duties not judicial in their nature; and they expressed their views in various ways.

In one circuit, the judges thinking it improper to act under this statute in their judicial capacity, for the reason above-named, consented from charitable motives to serve as " commissioners." [1]

debted to the courtesy of Dr. J. S. Billings, the Director of the New York Public Library, and the investigations of Mr. V. H. Paltsits, one of the librarians in that institution.

[1] This construction, that the statute purported to au-

In the Pennsylvania circuit, the three judges wrote, in a letter to the President, that " on a late painful occasion " they had held the law invalid ; and they now stated the matter to him, as being the person charged with the duty of "taking care that the laws be faithfully executed." They assured him that while this judicial action of disregarding an act of Congress had been necessary, it was far from pleasant.

The judges of another circuit, before which no case had come, wrote a similar letter to the President, declaring their reasons for thinking the law invalid.

In this same year, 1792, the Pennsylvania case came regularly up to the Supreme Court, and was argued there.[1] This might have produced a decision, but none was ever given ; and in the next year a change in the statute provided relief for the pension claimants in another way.

It is to be remarked, then, that this mat-

thorize their acting in that capacity was afterwards, in 1794, held by the Supreme Court to be wrong. Yale Todd's Case, 13 Howard, 52.

[1] Hayburn's Case, 2 Dallas, 409.

ter resulted in no decision by the Supreme
Court of the United States on the question
of the constitutionality of the pension act;
it produced only a decision at one of the
circuits, and informal expressions of opinion
from most of the judges.

These non-judicial communications of
opinion to the President seem, as has been
said, to have proceeded on the theory of fur-
nishing information to one whose official
duty it was to see that the fundamental law
was faithfully carried out; just as " Coun-
cils of Revision," established by the constitutions of Pennsylvania and Vermont, were
to report periodically as to infractions of
the constitution.

It was, perhaps, these practices of private
communication between the President and
the judges that led very soon to another
interesting matter, — a formal request by
the President, in 1793, for an opinion from
the judges on twenty-nine questions relating
to the treaties with France.  This request
accorded with a colonial practice of asking
such opinions from judges; a usage centu-

ries old in England, and preserved to-day in the constitutions of a few States in this country. The judges, however, declined answering these questions, "considering themselves," says Marshall, in his "Life of Washington," "merely as constituting a legal tribunal for the decision of controversies brought before them in legal form."[1] Although this seems to have been obviously the right course, since the proposition to give power to put questions to the judges in this way had been considered in the Federal Convention and not allowed, yet we may remark how convenient such a power would often have proved. If it be admitted, as it always has been in England, and is, almost universally, here, that such opinions are merely learned advice and bind nobody, not even the judges, they would often afford the executive and Congress much needed and early help upon constitutional questions in serious emergencies ; such, for example, as have lately presented themselves in our own history.

[1] Volume v., p. 444 (Philadelphia edition, 1807).

After this, there was an occasional allu-
sion in the opinions of the Supreme Court
to the question of the power of that court
to pass on the constitutionality of Federal
enactments as being an undecided and more
or less doubtful question. But not until
1803, early in Marshall's time, was the
point judicially presented to the Supreme
Court. It came up in the case of Marbury v. Madison,[1] the first case at the third
term after any opinions of Marshall were
reported. In that case, an act of Congress
was declared unconstitutional.

It was more than half a century before
that happened again.

Marbury v. Madison was a remarkable
case. It was connected intimately with certain executive action for which Marshall as
Secretary of State was partly responsible.
For various reasons the case must have ex-
cited peculiar interest in his mind. Within
three weeks before the end of Adams's administration, on February 13, 1801, while
Marshall was both Chief Justice and Secre-

[1] 1 Cranch, 137.

tary of State,[1] an act of Congress had abolished the old system of circuit and district courts, and established a new one. This gave to the President, Adams, the appointment of many new judges, and kept him and his secretary busy, during the last hours of the administration, in choosing and commissioning the new officials.

And another thing. The Supreme Court had consisted heretofore of six judges. This same act provided that after the next vacancy there should be five judges only. Such arrangements as these, made by a party just going out of power, were not ill calculated to create, in the mind of the party coming in, the impression of an intention to keep control of the judiciary as long as possible.

There were, to be sure, other reasons for some of this action. Several judges of the Supreme Court, as we have seen, had signified to Washington, in 1790, the opinion

[1] In like manner, Jay, commissioned Chief Justice on September 26, 1789, continued, at Washington's request, to act also as foreign secretary until Jefferson's return from Europe. Jefferson did not reach New York until March 21, 1790.

that the judiciary act of the previous year
was unconstitutional in making the judges
of that court judges also of the circuit court.
The new statute corrected this fault.    Yet,
in regard to the time chosen for this very
proper action, it was observable that ten
years and more had been allowed to pass
before the mischief so promptly pointed out
by the early judges was corrected.

Again, in approaching the case of Marbury *v.* Madison, it is to be observed that
another matter relating to the Supreme
Court had been dealt with.    This act of
February 13, 1801, provided that the two
terms of the court, instead of being held, as
hitherto, in February and August, should
thereafter be held in June and December.
Accordingly, the court sat in December,
1801.    It adjourned, as it imagined, to
June, 1802.    But, on March 8 of that year,
Congress, under the new administration,
repealed the law of 1801, unseated all the
new judges, and reinstated the old system,
with its August and February terms.    And
then, a little later in the year, the August

term of the court was abolished, leaving
only one term a year, to begin on the first
Monday in February. Thus, since the June
term was abolished, and February had then
passed, and there was no longer an August
or a December term, the court found itself
in effect adjourned by Congress from December, 1801, to February, 1803 ; and so it
had no session during the whole of the year
1802.

If the legislation of 1801 was calculated
to show the importance attached by an out-
going political party to control over the
judiciary, that of 1802 might indicate how
entirely the incoming party agreed with them,
and how well inclined they were to profit by
their own opportunities.

How was it, meantime, with the judiciary
itself ?    Unfortunately, the Supreme Court
had already been drawn into the quarrel.
For, at the single December term, in 1801,
held under the statute of that year, an application had been made to the court by four
persons in the District of Columbia for a
rule upon James Madison, Secretary of

State, to show cause why a writ of mandamus should not issue requiring him to issue
to these persons certain commissions as justice of the peace, which had been left in
Marshall's office undelivered at the time
when he ceased to add to his present functions those of Secretary of State. They had
been made out, sealed, and signed, and were
supposed to have been found by Madison
when he came into office, and to be now
withheld by him. This motion was pending
when the court adjourned, in December,
1801. Of course, a motion for a mandamus
to the head of the cabinet, upon a matter of
burning interest, must have attracted no little attention on the part of the new administration. Abolishing the August term served
to postpone any opportunity for early action
by the court, and to remind the judiciary of
the limits of its power.

At last the court came together, in February, 1803, and found the mandamus case
awaiting its action. It is the first one reported at that term. Since Marshall had
taken his seat, there had as yet been only

five reported cases. All the opinions had
been given by him, unless a few lines " by the
court " may be an exception ; and according
to the new usage by which the Chief Justice became, wherever it was possible, the
sole organ of the court, Marshall now gave
the opinion in Marbury *v.* Madison. It
may reasonably be wondered that the Chief
Justice should have been willing to give the
opinion in such a case, and especially that
he should have handled the case as he did.
But he was sometimes curiously regardless
of conventions.

If it be asked what was decided in Marbury *v.* Madison, the answer is that this,
and only this, was decided, namely, that the
court had no jurisdiction to do what they
were asked to do in that case (*i. e.* to grant
a writ of mandamus, in the exercise of their
original jurisdiction), because the Constitution allowed to the court no such power ; and,
although an act of Congress had undertaken
to confer this jurisdiction on them, Congress
had no power to do it, and therefore the act
was void, and must be disregarded by the

court.[1]   It is the decision upon this point
that makes the case famous; and undoubt-
edly it was reached in the legitimate exercise of the court's power.   To this important
part of the case attention will be called in
the next chapter.

Unfortunately, instead of proceeding as
courts usually do, the opinion began by
passing upon all the points which the denial
of its own jurisdiction took from it the right
to treat.   It was elaborately laid down, in
about twenty pages, out of the total twenty-
seven which comprise the opinion, that Madison had no right to detain the commissions;
and that mandamus would be the proper
remedy in any court which had jurisdiction
to grant it.

And thus, as the court, by its decision in
this case, was sharply reminding the legislature of its limitations, so by its *dicta*, and
in this irregular method, it intimated to the
President, also, that his department was not
exempt from judicial control.   In this way

[1] And so the careful headnote of Judge Curtis in 1
Curtis's *Decisions of the Supreme Court*, 368.

two birds were neatly reached with the same stone.

Marshall made a very noticeable remark in his opinion, seeming to point to the chief executive himself, and not merely to his secretary, when he said, " It is not the office of the person to whom the writ is directed, but the nature of the thing to be done, by which the propriety or impropriety of issuing the mandamus is to be determined ; " — a hint that, on an appropriate occasion, the judiciary might issue orders personally to him.   This remark got illustration a few years later, in 1807, when the Chief Justice, at the trial of Aaron Burr in Richmond, ordered a subpœna to the same President, Thomas Jefferson, directing him to bring thither certain documents.   It was a strange conception of the relations of the different departments of the government to each other, to imagine that a subpœna, that is to say an order accompanied with a threat of punishment, was a legitimate judicial mode of communicating with the chief executive.   On Jefferson's part, this order

was received with the utmost discontent;
and justly. He had a serious apprehension
of a purpose to arrest him by force, and
was prepared to protect himself.[1] Meantime he sent to the United States Attorney
at Richmond the papers called for, but explained, with dignity, that while the executive was willing to testify in Washington, it
could not allow itself to be " withdrawn
from its station by any coördinate authority."

It was partly to the tendency on Marshall's part, just mentioned, to give little
thought, often, to ordinary conventions, and
partly to his kindness of heart, that we
should attribute another singular occurrence,
— the fact that he attended a dinner at the
house of an old friend, one of Burr's counsel, when he knew that Burr was to be present, and when that individual, having previously been brought to Richmond under
arrest, examined by Marshall, and admitted
to bail, was still awaiting the action of the
grand jury with reference to further judicial

[1] See Ford's *Jefferson*, ix. 62; draft of a letter to District Attorney Hay.

proceedings before Marshall himself.   He
accepted the invitation before he knew that
Burr was to be of the company.   I have
heard from one of his descendants that
his wife advised him not to go; but he
thought it best not to seem too fastidious, or
to appear to censure his old friend, the host,
by staying away.   He sat, we are told, at
the opposite end of the table from Burr,
had no communication with him, and went
away early.   But we must still wonder at an
act which he himself afterwards much regretted.

# CHAPTER IV

## MARSHALL'S CONSTITUTIONAL OPINIONS

THIS is not the place for any detailed
consideration of Marshall's decisions. But
it would be a strange omission to leave out
all consideration of what played so great a
part in his life. I must draw, therefore,
upon the patience of the reader, while some
points are mentioned relating to that class
of his opinions which is at once the most
important and of the widest interest, viz.,
those given in constitutional cases. If these
matters seem to any reader dull or unintelli-
gible, he must be allowed full liberty to pass
them by; but I cannot wholly omit them.

The keynote to Marshall's leading constitutional opinions is that of giving free
scope to the power of the national government. These leading opinions may be
divided into three classes: *First*, such as
discuss the nature and reach of the Federal

Constitution, and the general relation of the federal government to the States. Of this class, McCulloch *v.* Maryland, probably his greatest opinion, is the chief illustration. *Second*, those cases which are concerned with the specific restraints and limitations upon the States. To this class may be assigned Fletcher *v.* Peck, the bankruptcy cases of Sturgis *v.* Crowninshield and Ogden *v.* Saunders, and Dartmouth College *v.* Woodward. *Third*, such as deal with the general theory and principles of constitutional law. There is little of this sort; except as it is incidentally touched, perhaps the only case is Marbury *v.* Madison.

If we look at these great cases merely with reference to their effect upon the history and development of the country, they are of the very first importance. When one names Marbury *v.* Madison, the first case where the Supreme Court held an act of Congress invalid, and the only one in Marshall's time; Fletcher *v.* Peck and Dartmouth College *v.* Woodward, where legislative grants and an act of incorporation are held to be contracts, protected by the United States Constitution against state legislation impairing their obligation; and New Jersey *v.* Wilson, holding that a legislative exemption from taxation is also a contract protected in the same way; — one sees the tremendous importance of the decisions.

Of course we are not to confound this powerful effect of a judgment, or the moral approbation with which we may be inclined to view it, with the intrinsic merit of the reasoning or the legal soundness of the conclusions. It is not uncommon to speak of the reasoning in Marbury *v.* Madison and Dartmouth College *v.* Woodward with the greatest praise. But neither of these opinions is entitled to rank with Marshall's greatest work. The very common view to which I have alluded is partly referable to the fallacy which Wordsworth once remarked upon when a friend mentioned " The Happy Warrior " as being the greatest of his poems. " No," said the poet, " you are mistaken; your judgment is affected by your moral approval of the lines."

If we regard at once the greatness of the questions at issue in the particular case, the influence of the opinion, and the large method and clear and skillful manner in which it is worked out, there is nothing so fine as the opinion in McCulloch v. Maryland, given at the February term, 1819. The questions were, first, whether the United States could constitutionally incorporate a bank; and, second, if it could, whether a State might tax the operations of the bank; as, in this instance, by requiring it to use stamped paper for its notes. The bank was sustained and the tax condemned.

In working this out, it was laid down that while the United States is merely a government of enumerated powers, and these do not in terms include the granting of an incorporation, yet it is a government whose powers, though limited in number, are in general supreme, and also adequate to the great national purposes for which they are given; that these great purposes carry with them the power of adopting such means, not prohibited by the Constitution, as are fairly conducive to the end ; and that incorporating a bank is not forbidden, and is useful for several ends. Further, the paramount relation of the national government, whose valid laws the Constitution makes the supreme law of the land, forbids the States to tax, or to " retard, impede, burden, or in any way control " the operations of the government in any of its instrumentalities.

This was the opinion of a unanimous court, in which five out of the seven judges had been nominated by a Republican President. But it caused great excitement at the South. On March 24, 1819, Marshall wrote from Richmond to Judge Story : " Our opinion in the bank case has roused the sleeping spirit of Virginia, if indeed it ever sleeps. It will, I understand, be attacked in the papers with some asperity, and as those who favor it never write for the public it will remain undefended, and of course be considered as *damnably heretical*." Again, two months later, " The opinion in the bank case continues to be denounced by the Democracy of Virginia. . . . If the prin-

ciples which have been advanced on this
occasion were to prevail the Constitution
would be converted into the old Confederation."

Another great opinion, of the same class,
and also bitterly attacked, was given in the
case of Cohens v. Virginia, in 1821. This
case came up on a writ of error from a local
court at Norfolk. Cohens had been con-
victed of selling lottery tickets there, contrary to the statute of Virginia. He had set
up as a defense an act of Congress provid-
ing for drawing lotteries in the city of
Washington, and insisted that this authorized his selling tickets in Virginia. When
the case reached the Supreme Court of the
United States, the counsel for the State first
denied the jurisdiction of that court, on the
ground, among others, that the Constitution
allowed no such appeal from a state court,
and that the Judiciary Act of 1789 was unconstitutional in purporting to authorize it.
In an elaborate opinion by Marshall, one of
his greatest efforts, these contentions were
negatived. When afterwards, the case came

to be argued on the merits, the decision below was sustained, on the ground that the act of Congress did not purport to authorize the sale of tickets in any State which forbade the sale of them.

Here again the court was unanimous; and it was composed of the same judges who decided McCulloch v. Maryland. But the reception of Cohens v. Virginia at the South was even worse than that accorded the other case. Judge Roane, of the Court of Appeals in Virginia, attacked the opinion anonymously in the newspapers, with what Marshall called "coarseness and malignity." Jefferson, also, bitterly objected to it.

Of two other cases belonging in the same class of Marshall's opinions, viz., Gibbons v. Ogden, in 1824, and Brown v. Maryland, in 1827, it is enough here to say that they deal with one of the most difficult and perplexed topics of constitutional law, namely, the coördination of the functions of the national and state governments, in regard to the power granted to Congress to regulate foreign and interstate commerce, a subject of great importance and difficulty, on which the decisions of the Supreme Court are now and long have been involved in much confusion and uncertainty. Gibbons *v.* Ogden brought into question the constitutionality of a law of New York granting to Fulton, the inventor, the sole right of navigating the waters of New York by steam. The grant had been sustained by Chancellor Kent and by the New York Court of Appeals; but these decisions were now overruled in a famous and powerful opinion. In two other cases on this subject, also of great importance, Marshall gave leading opinions. It may fairly be thought that his treatment of the general question involved in these cases, instructive as it was, was yet less fruitful and less far-seeing than in most of his other great cases.

He was now in a region pretty closely connected with the second class of cases, above named; a set of cases, where even so great a man as Marshall erred sometimes, from interpreting too literally and too narrowly the restraints upon the States. It was

natural, in giving full scope to the authority
of the general government, that he should
be inclined to apply, with their fullest force
and operation, these clauses of restraint and
prohibition.   His great service to the country and his own generation was that of
planting the national government on the
broadest and strongest foundations.   That,
as he rightly conceived, was the one chief
necessity of his time.   In doing this, when
it came to considering the reach that must
also be allowed to the States, and just how
the coördination of the two systems should
be worked out, probably no one man, no
one court, no human wisdom was adequate,
then, to mapping it all out.   Time alone,
and a long succession of men, after some
ages of experience, might suffice for that.
The wisdom of those who made the Constitution, as it has lately been said, was mainly
shown " in the shortness and generality of
its provisions, in its silence, and its abstinence from petty limitations."   But, as time
went on, definitions and specifications had to
be made and applied ; silence, abstinence,

generality, were no longer adequate. And in the class of cases, now referred to, great and far-reaching as were the results of Marshall's labor, and unqualifiedly as they are often praised, one may perceive, as I venture to think, a less comprehensive and statesmanlike grasp of the problems and their essential conditions than are found in some other parts of his work.

And so, when the Chief Justice, in 1812, held, without argument, that a grant of land by a State, with a privilege of exemption from taxation, contained a contract against future taxation, protected, even in the hands of subsequent holders, by the constitutional provisions against impairing the obligation of contracts, something was done which would probably not be done to-day, if the question came up for the first time. Certainly the soundness of the doctrine has been frequently denied by judges of the Supreme court, and it has only survived through the device of construing all grants in the narrowest manner. " Yielding," says the Court in a recent case, " to the doctrine that im-

munity from taxation may be granted, that
point being already adjudged, it must be
considered as a personal privilege, not extending beyond the immediate grantee, unless otherwise so declared in express terms."
And again the court has recently remarked
on the "well-settled rule that exemptions
from taxation are . . . not to be extended
beyond the exact and express language used,
construed *strictissimi juris*."

Again, in Dartmouth College *v.* Woodward, in 1819, when it was held that a legislative grant of incorporation was a contract
protected by the same clause of the Constitution, something was done from which the
court was subsequently obliged to recede in
an important degree.   Acts of incorporation
for the manufacture of beer, for carrying on
slaughter-houses, for dealing in offal, and
for conducting a lottery, — a reputable business in 1819, when the Dartmouth College
case was decided, — such acts as these have
been treated by the Supreme Court as not
being thus protected.   It is held that no
legislative body can contract to part with

the full power to provide for the health, morals, and safety of the community. Such things, it is said, are not the proper subject-matter of legislative contract, — a doctrine which it has been widely thought should, originally, have been applied to all acts of incorporation. " The State," says a distinguished judge, and writer on constitutional law, in speaking of the Dartmouth College doctrine and its development, " was stripped, under this interpretation, of prerogatives that are commonly regarded as inseparable from sovereignty, and might have stood, like Lear, destitute before her offspring, had not the police power been dexterously declared paramount, and used as a means of rescinding improvident grants." [1]

In the great bankruptcy cases of Sturgis *v.* Crowninshield and Ogden *v.* Saunders, where it was held, in 1819 and 1827, that the constitutional provision as to impairing the obligation of contracts forbade the State to enact an insolvency law which should discharge a person from liability on a

[1] Hare, Am. Const. Law, i. 607.

contract made before the law; and then
again that it did not forbid the same thing
as touching a contract made after the law,
Marshall, who gave the opinion in the first
case, put it on a ground equally applicable
to the second; and so, in the second case,
gave a dissenting opinion. The obligation
of the contract, he said, comes from the
agreement of the party; it does not arise
from the law of the State at the time it was
made, entering into or operating on the contract. But this doctrine and this reasoning
were justly disallowed.

Finally, in 1830, in Craig *v.* Missouri,
Marshall gave the opinion that certain cer-
tificates issued by a State in return for depos-
its, and intended to circulate as money, were
bills of credit; and as such forbidden by
the Constitution. There were three dissenting opinions; and soon after Marshall's
death,. a different doctrine was established
by the court, — wisely it would seem, — and
has ever since been maintained.[1]

Coming now to the third class of cases

[1] See, however, Chancellor Kent in 2 N. Y. Rev. 372.

mentioned above, that which deals with the fundamental conceptions and theory of our American doctrine of constitutional law, Marbury *v.* Madison is the chief case. In speaking of that case I have purposely delayed until this point any reference to this aspect of it. While, historically, this part of it is what gives the case its chief importance, yet it occupies only about a quarter of the opinion.

In outline, the argument there presented is as follows: The question is whether a court can give effect to an unconstitutional act of the legislature. This question is answered, as having little difficulty, by referring to a few " principles long and well established." (1) The people, in establishing a written constitution and limiting the powers of the legislature, intend to control it; else the legislature could change the constitution by an ordinary act. (2) If a superior law is not thus changeable, then an unconstitutional act is not law. This theory, it is added, is essentially attached to a written constitution. (3) If the act is void, it

cannot bind the court. The court has to
say what the law is, and in saying this must
judge between the Constitution and the act.
Otherwise, a void act would be obligatory;
and this would be saying that constitutional
limits upon legislation may be transgressed
by the legislature at pleasure, and thus these
limits would be reduced to nothing. (4) The
language of the Federal instrument gives
judicial power in " cases arising under the
Constitution." Judges are thus in terms referred to the Constitution. They are sworn
to support it and cannot violate it. And so,
it is said, in conclusion, the peculiar phrase-
ology of the instrument confirms what is
supposed to be essential to all written constitutions, that a law repugnant to it is void,
and that the courts, as well as other departments, are bound by the constitution.

The reasoning is mainly that of Hamilton, in his short essay of a few years before
in the " Federalist." The short and dry
treatment of the subject, as being one of
no real difficulty, is in sharp contrast with
the protracted reasoning of McCulloch v.

Maryland, Cohens *v.* Virginia, and other great cases; and this treatment is much to be regretted. Absolutely settled as the general doctrine is to-day, and sound as it is, when regarded as a doctrine for the descendants of British colonists, there are grave and far-reaching considerations — such, too, as affect to-day the proper administration of this extremely important power — which are not touched by Marshall, and which must have commanded his attention if the subject had been deeply considered and fully expounded according to his later method. His reasoning does not answer the difficulties that troubled Swift, afterwards chief justice of Connecticut, and Gibson, afterwards chief justice of Pennsylvania, and many other strong, learned, and thoughtful men; not to mention Jefferson's familiar and often ill-digested objections.

It assumes as an essential feature of a written constitution what does not exist in any one of the written constitutions of Europe. It does not remark the grave dis-

tinction between the power of disregarding
the act of a coördinate department, and the
action of a federal court in dealing thus
with the legislation of the local States; a
distinction important in itself, and observed
under the written constitutions of Europe,
which, as I have said, allow this power in
the last sort of case, while denying it in the
other.

Had Marshall dealt with this subject after
the fashion of his greatest opinions he must
also have considered and passed upon certain serious suggestions arising out of the
arrangements of our own constitutions and
the exigencies of the different departments.
All the departments, and not merely the
judges, are sworn to support the Constitution. All are bound to decide for themselves, in the first instance, what this instrument requires of them. None can have help
from the courts unless, in course of time,
some litigated case should arise; and of
some questions it is true that they never
can arise in the way of litigation. What
was Andrew Johnson to do when the Recon-

struction Acts of 1867 had been passed over his veto by the constitutional majority, while his veto had gone on the express ground, still held by him, that they were unconstitutional? He had sworn to support the Constitution. Should he execute an enactment which was contrary to the Constitution, and so void? Or should he say, as he did say to the court, through his Attorney-General, that "from the moment [these laws] were passed over his veto, there was but one duty, in his estimation, resting upon him, and that was faithfully to carry out and execute these laws"?[1]   And why is he to say this?

Again, what is the House of Representatives to do when a treaty, duly made and ratified by the constitutional authority, namely, the President and Senate, comes before it for an appropriation of money to carry it out? Has the House, under these circumstances, anything to do with the question of constitutionality? If it thinks the treaty unconstitutional, and so void, can it

[1] Mississippi v. Johnson, 4 Wallace, 475, 492 (1866).

vote to carry it out?   If it can, how is this justified?

Is the situation necessarily different when a court is asked to enforce a legislative act? The courts are not strangers to the case of political questions, where they must refuse to interfere with the acts of the other departments, — as in the case relating to Andrew Johnson just referred to ; and in dealing with what are construed to be merely directory provisions of the Constitution ; and with the cases, well approved in the Supreme Court of the United States, where courts refuse to consider whether provisions of a constitution have been complied with, which require certain formalities in passing laws, — accepting as final the certificate of the officers of the political departments.   A question, passed upon by those departments, is thus refused any discussion in the judicial forum, on the ground, to quote the language of the Supreme Court, that " the respect due to coequal and independent departments requires the judicial department to act upon this assurance."

So far as any necessary conclusion is concerned, it might fairly have been said, with us, as it is said in Europe, that the real question in all these cases is not whether the act is constitutional, but whether its constitutionality can properly be brought in question before a given tribunal. Could Marshall have had to deal with this great question, in answer to Chief Justice Gibson's powerful opinion in Eakin *v.* Raub, in 1825,[1] instead of deciding it without being helped or hindered by any adverse argument at all, as he did, we should have had a far higher exhibition of his powers than the case now affords.[2]

[1] 12 Serg. & Rawle, 330; s. c. 1 Thayer's Const. Cases, 133.

[2] As to this general subject see " Origin and Scope of the American Doctrine of Constitutional Law," 7 *Harvard Law Review*, 129. Compare the remark of Lord John Russell : " Every political constitution, in which different bodies share the supreme power, is only enabled to exist by the forbearance of those among whom this power is distributed." I quote this from the motto of Woodrow Wilson's fifth chapter in his *Congressional Government.*

# CHAPTER V

I HAVE drawn attention to the immense
service that Chief Justice Marshall rendered
to his country in the field of constitutional
law, and have considered a few of the cases.
Since his time not twice the length of his
term of thirty-four years has gone by, but
more than five times the number of volumes that sufficed for the opinions of the
Supreme Court during his period is required
for those of his successors on the bench.
Nor does even that proportion indicate the
increase in the quantity of the court's business which is referable to this particular
part of the law. It has enormously increased. When one reflects upon the multi-
tude, variety, and complexity of the questions relating to the regulation of interstate
commerce, upon the portentous and ever

increasing flood of litigation to which the
Fourteenth Amendment has given rise;
upon the new problems in business, government, and police which have come in with
steam and electricity, and their ten thousand applications ; upon the growth of cor-
porations and of wealth, the changes of
opinion on social questions, such as the relation of capital and labor, and upon the
recent expansions of our control over great
and distant islands, — we seem to be living
in a different world from Marshall's.

Under these new circumstances, what is
happening in the region of constitutional
law? Very serious things, indeed.

The people of the States, when making
new constitutions, have long been adding
more and more prohibitions and restraints
upon their legislatures. The courts, meantime, in many places, enter into the harvest
thus provided for them with a light heart,
and too promptly and easily proceed to set
aside legislative acts. The legislatures are
growing accustomed to this distrust, and
more and more readily incline to justify it,

and to shed the consideration of constitutional restraints, — certainly as concerning
the exact extent of these restrictions, — turning that subject over to the courts; and,
what is worse, they insensibly fall into a
habit of assuming that whatever they can
constitutionally do they may do, — as if honor
and fair dealing and common honesty were
not relevant to their inquiries.

The people, all this while, become careless as to whom they send to the legislature;
too often they cheerfully vote for men whom
they would not trust with an important private affair, and when these unfit persons
are found to pass foolish and bad laws, and
the courts step in and disregard them, the
people are glad that these few wiser gentlemen on the bench are so ready to protect
them against their more immediate representatives.

From these causes there has developed a
vast and growing increase of judicial interference with legislation.   This is a very different state of things from what our fathers
contemplated, a century and more ago, in

framing the new system.  Seldom, indeed,
as they imagined, under our system, would
this great, novel, tremendous power of the
courts be exerted, — would this sacred ark
of the covenant be taken from within the
veil.  Marshall himself expressed truly one
aspect of the matter, when he said in one of
the later years of his life: "No questions
can be brought before a judicial tribunal of
greater delicacy than those which involve
the constitutionality of legislative acts.  If
they become indispensably necessary to the
case, the court must meet and decide them ;
but if the case may be determined on other
grounds, a just respect for the legislature
requires that the obligation of its laws
should not be unnecessarily and wantonly
assailed."  And again, a little earlier than
this, he laid down the one true rule of duty
for the courts.  When he went to Philadelphia at the end of September, in 1831, on
that painful errand of which I have spoken,
in answering a cordial tribute from the bar
of that city he remarked that if he might be
permitted to claim for himself and his asso-

ciates any part of the kind things they had said, it would be this, that they had "never sought to enlarge the judicial power beyond its proper bounds, nor feared to carry it to the fullest extent that duty required."

That is the safe twofold rule ; nor is the first part of it any whit less important than the second ; nay, more ; to-day it is the part which most requires to be emphasized.   For just here comes in a consideration of very great weight.   Great and, indeed, inestimable as are the advantages in a popular government of this conservative influence, — the power of the judiciary to disregard unconstitutional legislation, — it should be remembered that the exercise of it, even when unavoidable, is always attended with a serious evil, namely, that the correction of legislative mistakes comes from the outside, and the people thus lose the political experience, and the moral education and stimulus that come from fighting the question out in the ordinary way, and correcting their own errors. If the decision in Munn *v.* Illinois and the " Granger Cases," twenty-five years ago, and

in the " Legal Tender Cases," nearly thirty
years ago, had been different; and the legislation there in question, thought by many to
be unconstitutional and by many more to be
ill-advised, had been set aside, we should have
been saved some trouble and some harm.   But
I venture to think that the good which came
to the country and its people from the vigorous thinking that had to be done in the political debates that followed, from the infiltra-
tion through every part of the population of
sound ideas and sentiments, from the rous-
ing into activity of opposite elements, the
enlargement of ideas, the strengthening of
moral fibre, and the growth of political experience that came out of it all, — that all
this far more than outweighed any evil which
ever flowed from the refusal of the court to
interfere with the work of the legislature.

The tendency of a common and easy resort
to this great function, now lamentably too
common, is to dwarf the political capacity of
the people, and to deaden its sense of moral
responsibility.   It is no light thing to do
that.

What can be done? It is the courts that
can do most to cure the evil; and the opportunity is a very great one. Let them
resolutely adhere to first principles. Let
them consider how narrow is the function
which the constitutions have conferred on
them, — the office merely of deciding litigated cases; how large, therefore, is the
duty intrusted to others, and above all to
the legislature. It is that body which is
charged, primarily, with the duty of judging
of the constitutionality of its work. The
constitutions generally give them no authority to call upon a court for advice; they
must decide for themselves, and the courts
may never be able to say a word. Such a
body, charged, in every State, with almost all
the legislative power of the people, is entitled to the most entire and real respect; is
entitled, as among all rationally permissible
opinions as to what the constitution allows,
to its own choice. Courts, as has often been
said, are not to think of the legislators, but
of the legislature, — the great, continuous
body itself, abstracted from all the transi-

tory individuals who may happen to hold its
power.   It is this majestic representative of
the people whose action is in question, a
coördinate department of the government,
charged with the greatest functions, and in-
vested, in contemplation of law, with what-
soever wisdom, virtue, and knowledge the
exercise of such functions requires.

To set aside the acts of such a body, repre-
senting in its own field, which is the very
highest of all, the ultimate sovereign, should
be a solemn, unusual, and painful act.  Something is wrong when it can ever be other
than that.   And if it be true that the holders of legislative power are careless or evil,
yet the constitutional duty of the court remains untouched; it cannot rightly attempt
to protect the people, by undertaking a function not its own.  On the other hand, by ad-
hering rigidly to its own duty, the court will
help, as nothing else can, to fix the spot where
responsibility lies, and to bring down on that
precise locality the thunderbolt of popular
condemnation.    The judiciary, to-day, in
dealing with the acts of their coördinate

legislators, owe to the country no greater or
clearer duty than that of keeping their hands
off these acts wherever it is possible to do
it. For that course — the true course of
judicial duty always — will powerfully help
to bring the people and their representatives to a sense of their own responsibility.
There will still remain to the judiciary an
ample field for the determinations of this
remarkable jurisdiction, of which our American law has so much reason to be proud ; a
jurisdiction which has had some of its chief
illustrations and its greatest triumphs, as in
Marshall's time, so in ours, while the courts
were refusing to exercise it.

## CHAPTER VI

No systematic attempt seems ever to have been made to collect Marshall's letters. It should be done. Only a few of his family letters have yet found their way into print. One of them, to his wife, is quoted in a previous page. In another to her, written on March 9, 1825, referring to the inauguration of President John Quincy Adams, he says: "I administered the oath to the President in the presence of an immense concourse of people, in my new suit of domestic manufacture. He, too, was dressed in the same manner, though his clothes were made at a different establishment. The cloth is very fine and smooth."

In a letter of December 7, 1834,[1] to his grandson, "Mr. John Marshall, jr.," he gives the boy some advice about writing

[1] *The Nation*, February 7, 1901.

which is a good commentary on the extraordinary neatness and felicity, the close
fit, of his own clear, compact, and simple
style : —

" The man who by seeking embellishment
hazards confusion is greatly mistaken in what
constitutes good writing.  The meaning ought
never to be mistaken.  Indeed, the readers
should never be obliged to search for it.
The writer should always express himself so
clearly as to make it impossible to misun-
derstand him.  He should be comprehended
without an effort.  The first step towards
writing and speaking clearly is to think
clearly.  Let the subject be perfectly understood, and a man will soon find words to
convey his meaning to others."

A letter to James Monroe, dated Richmond, December 2, 1784, was written while
Marshall was a member of the House of
Delegates.  He writes : " Not a bill of public importance, in which an individual was
not particularly interested, has passed.  The
exclusive privilege given to Rumsey and his
assigns to build and navigate his new in-

vented boats is of as much, perhaps more, consequence than any other bill we have passed. We have rejected some which, in my conception, would have been advantageous to this country. Among these I rank the bill for encouraging intermarriage with the Indians. Our prejudices, however, oppose themselves to our interests, and operate too powerfully for them. . . .

"I shewed my father [then, probably, living in Kentucky] that part of your letter which respects the western country. He says he will render you every service of the kind you mention which is within his power with a great deal of pleasure. He says, though, that Mr. Humphrey Marshall, a cousin and brother of mine,[1] is better acquainted with the lands and would be better enabled to choose for your advantage than he would. If, however, you wish rather to depend on my father I presume he may avail himself of the knowledge of his son-in-law. I do not know what to say to your scheme of selling out. If you can execute it you will

[1] He married John Marshall's sister.

have made a very capital sum; if you can
retain your lands you will be poor during
life unless you remove to the western country, but you will have secured for posterity
an immense fortune. I should prefer the
selling business, and if you adopt it I think
you have fixed on a very proper price.

"Adieu.   May you be very happy is the
wish of your            J. MARSHALL."

In another letter to Monroe, while the
latter was Madison's Secretary of State,
dated Richmond, June 25, 1812, just as the
war was beginning, he says: —

"On my return to-day from my farm,
where I pass a considerable portion of my
time in *laborious relaxation*, I found a
copy of the message of the President, of
the 1st inst., accompanied by the report
of the Committee of Foreign Relations and
the declaration of war against Britain, under
cover from you.

"Permit me to subjoin to my thanks for
this mark of your attention my fervent wish
that this momentous measure may, in its

operation on the interest and honor of our country, disappoint only its enemies.

" Whether my prayer be heard or not, I shall remain with respectful esteem,

" Your obedient servant,

" J. MARSHALL."

When Marshall went to France as envoy in 1797, he wrote several long and interesting letters to Washington, acquainting him with whatever foreign intelligence might interest him.[1] The following passages from the first letter, a very long one, will show the interest of these papers, and the exactness of the information they convey : —

" THE HAGUE, 15th Sept., 1797.

" DEAR SIR, — The flattering evidences I have received of your favorable opinion, which have made on my mind an impression only to wear out with my being, added to a conviction that you must feel a deep interest in all that concerns a country to

[1] These letters were printed in 1897 in the *American Hist. Review*, ii. 294.   I was not aware of their ever having been printed, until after these pages were in type.

whose service you have devoted so large a
portion of your life, induce me to offer you
such occasional communications as, while in
Europe, I may be enabled to make, and induce a hope that the offer will not be
deemed an unacceptable or unwelcome intrusion.

" Until our arrival in Holland we saw
only British and neutral vessels. This added
to the blockade of the Dutch fleet in the
Texel, of the French fleet in Brest, and of
the Spanish fleet in Cadiz, manifests the entire dominion which one nation at present
possesses over the seas. By the ships of
war which met us we were three times
visited, and the conduct of those who came
on board was such as would proceed from
general orders to pursue a system calculated
to conciliate America. Whether this be
occasioned by a sense of justice and the obligations of good faith, or solely by the
hope that the perfect contrast which it exhibits to the conduct of France may excite
keener sensations at that conduct, its effects
on our commerce are the same.

" The situation of Holland is truly interesting.  Though the face of the country still
exhibits a degree of wealth and population
still unequaled in any part of Europe, its
decline is visible.  The great city of Amsterdam is in a state of blockade.  More than
two thirds of its shipping lie unemployed in
port.  Other seaports suffer, though not in
so great a degree.  In the mean time the
requisitions made upon them are enormous.
They have just completed the payment of the
100,000,000 of florins (equal to 40,000,000
of dollars) stipulated by treaty ; they have
sunk, on the first entrance of the French,
a very considerable sum in assignats ; they
made large contributions in specifics, and
they pay, feed, and clothe an army esti-
mated, as I am informed, at near three
times its real number.  It is supposed that
France has by various means drawn from
Holland about 60,000,000 of dollars.  This
has been paid, in addition to the natural
expenditures, by a population of less than
2,000,000.  Nor, should the war continue,
can the contributions of Holland stop here·

The increasing exigencies of France must inevitably increase her demands on those within her reach.

.    .    .    .    .    .    .    .

" The political opinions which have produced the rejection of the Constitution, and which, as it would seem, can only be entertained by intemperate and ill-informed minds, unaccustomed to a union of theory and practice of liberty, must be associated with a general system which if brought into action will produce the same excesses here which have been so justly deplored in France. The same materials exist, though not in so great a degree. They have their clubs, they have a numerous poor, and they have enormous wealth in the hands of a minority of the nation. On my remarking this to a very rich and intelligent merchant of Amsterdam, and observing that if one class of men withdrew itself from public duties and offices it would be immediately succeeded by another, which would acquire a degree of power and influence that might be exercised to the destruction of those who had retired

from society, he replied that the remark was
just, but that they relied ·on France for a
protection from those evils which she had
herself experienced.    That France would
continue to require great supplies from Holland, and knew its situation too well to permit it to become the prey of anarchy.    That
Holland was an artificial country acquired
by persevering industry, and which could
only be preserved by wealth and order.
That confusion and anarchy would banish a
large portion of that wealth, would dry up
its sources, and would entirely disable them
from giving France that pecuniary aid she
so much needed.    That under this impression many who, though friendly to the revolution, saw with infinite mortification French
troops garrison the towns of Holland, would
now see their departure with equal regret.
Thus they willingly relinquished national independence for individual safety.    What a
lesson to those who would admit foreign influence into the United States!".  .  .

The condition of affairs in Paris at that
time is illustrated by the fact that Marshall's

later letters, written from there, were not
signed ; and that they allude to the action of
himself and his associates in the third person. Thus, writing from Paris, October 24,
1797, in the character of an anonymous private American to an unnamed correspond-
ent, he says : —

" Causes which I am persuaded you have
anticipated forbid me to allow that free
range of thought and expression which could
alone apologize for the intrusive character
my letters bear. Having, however, offered
what I cannot furnish, I go on to substitute something else perhaps not worth receiving. . . .

" Our ministers have not yet, nor do they
seem to think it certain that they will be
received. Indeed they make arrangements
which denote an expectation of returning to
America immediately. The captures of our
vessels seem to be only limited by the ability
to capture. That ability is increasing, as
the government has let out to hardy adven-
turers the national frigates. Among those
who plunder us, who are most active in this

infamous business, and most loud in vocif-
erating criminations equally absurd and un-
true, are some unprincipled apostates who
were born in America.   The sea rovers by
a variety of means seem to have acquired
great influence in the government.   This influence will be exerted to prevent an accommodation between the United States and
France, and to prevent any regulations
which may intercept the passage of the
spoils they have made on our commerce, to
their pockets.   The government, I believe,
is but too well disposed to promote their
views."

In a letter to Judge Peters, of Philadelphia, dated November 23, 1807, just after
the Burr trial, after thanking his correspond-
ent for a volume of " Admiralty Reports,"
he has something to say of that case : —

" I have as yet been able only to peep
into the book, not to read many of the cases.
I received it while fatigued, and occupied
with the most unpleasant case which has
ever been brought before a judge in this or,
perhaps, in any other country which affected

to be governed by laws; since the decision
of which I have been entirely from home.
The day after the commitment of Colonel
Burr for a misdemeanor I galloped to the
mountains, whence I only returned in time
to perform my North Carolina circuit, which
terminates just soon enough to enable me to
be here to open the court for the ancient
dominion.    Thus you perceive I have sufficient bodily employment to prevent my mind
from perplexing itself about the attentions
paid me in Baltimore and elsewhere.   I wish
I could have had as fair an opportunity to
let the business go off as a jest here as you
seem to have had in Philadelphia; but it
was most deplorably serious, and I could not
give the subject a different aspect by treating it in any manner which was in my power.
I might, perhaps, have made it less serious
to myself by obeying the public will, instead
of the public law, and throwing a little more
of the sombre upon others."

## CHAPTER VII

MARSHALL AS A CITIZEN AND A NEIGHBOR

THERE is more to be said of Marshall's private and personal life. After he went on the bench, his principal non-judicial work, in the nature of public service, seems to have been writing the "Life of Washington," with the later revision and reconstruction of that work, and his activity in a few matters of not too partisan a sort, such as were likely to engage the attention of a public-spirited citizen.

In 1813, at a meeting of the citizens of Richmond, he was appointed member of a Committee of Vigilance, to aid in defending the city against attack from the British. On June 28 he made a report, for a sub-committee, that it was inexpedient to undertake to fortify the city. After stating the topographical and other reasons for such an opinion, the report goes on thus: " Your committee

are too conscious of their destitution of
professional skill to advance with any confidence the opinion they have formed; but
the resolution under which they act having
made it their duty to give an opinion, they
say, though with much diffidence, that they
do not think any attempt to fortify the city
advisable. It is to be saved by operations
in the open field, by facing the enemy with a
force which may deter him from any attempt
to penetrate the interior of our country, and
which may impress him with the danger of
separating himself from his ships. If this
protection cannot be afforded, Richmond
must share the fate of other places which
are in similar circumstances. Throughout
the world, open towns belong to the army
which is master of the country. . . . If the
militia be put into the best condition for
service, if the light artillery be well manned
and supplied with horses, so as to move with
celerity to any point where its services may
be required; if the cavalry be kept entire
and in active service; if the precaution of
supplying in sufficient quantity all the im-

plements of war be taken, your committtee
hope and believe that this town will have no
reason to fear the invading foe." [1]

In those efforts on the part of some of
the leaders of Virginia and the South, early
in the century, to rid themselves of slavery,
to which we at the North have never done
sufficient justice, Marshall took an active
part.

The American Colonization Society was
organized in 1816 or 1817, with Bushrod
Washington for president. In 1823 an aux-
iliary society was organized at Richmond, of
which Marshall was president, an office which
he held nearly or quite up to the time of his
death. It is interesting to observe that one
of the plans for colonization was to have
worked out the abolition of slavery in Virginia in the year 1901. Of slavery Marshall wrote to a friend, in 1826 : " I concur
with you in thinking that nothing portends
more calamity and mischief to the Southern
States than their slave population. Yet they
seem to cherish the evil, and to view with

[1] *The Virginia Magazine of History*, vii. 233.

immovable prejudice and dislike everything
which may tend to diminish it. I do not
wonder that they should resist any attempt,
should one be made, to interfere with the
rights of property, but they have a feverish
jealousy of measures which may do good
without the hazard of harm, that, I think,
very unwise."

In 1828, Marshall presided, in Virginia,
over a convention to promote internal im-
provements. On this subject he held and
freely expressed views, such as are now generally entertained, as to the power of the
general government, and the expediency of
exerting them.[1]

In 1829, he allowed himself to be elected
to the Virginia convention for revising the
state constitution, and took an active part in
the debates. "Tall, in a long surtout of
blue, with a face of genius and an eye of
fire," is the description that is given of him
in the convention. On several questions he
influenced greatly the course of the convention, especially in continuing, for a score of

[1] Chancellor Kent in *New York Review*, 348, 349.

years to come, the judicial tenure of office
during good behavior.

Marshall's membership of the society of
Free Masons is sometimes spoken of. It
should be said that he lived to condemn that
organization. During the political excitement which followed the abduction of Mor-
gan, he was asked for information as to
some praise of Freemasonry which had been
publicly attributed to him, and replied, in
October, 1833, that he was not particularly
interested in the anti-masonic excitement.
"The agitations which convulse the North
did not pass the Potomac. Consequently
. . . I felt no inclination to volunteer in a
distant conflict, in which the wounds that
might be received would not be soothed by
the consoling reflection that he suffered in
the performance of a necessary duty." And
he added that he had " never affirmed that
there was any positive good or ill in the
institution itself." This cautious letter is
illustrated by an earlier one, in July, 1833,
in which, writing confidentially to Edward
Everett, he says that he became a Mason

soon after he entered the army, and afterwards continued in the society because his
neighbors did.    " I followed the crowd for a
time, without attaching the least importance
to its object or giving myself the trouble to
inquire why others did.    It soon lost its
attraction, and though there are several
lodges in the city of Richmond, I have not
been in one of them for more than forty
years, except on an invitation to accompany
General Lafayette, nor have I been a member of one of them for more than thirty.    It
was impossible not to perceive the useless
pageantry of the whole exhibition."    And he
adds that he has become convinced " that
the institution ought to be abandoned, as
one capable of producing much evil and
incapable of producing any good which
might not be effected by safe and open
means." [1]

As to Marshall's religious affiliations, he
was a regular and devoted attendant, all his
life, of the Episcopal Church, in which he

[1] *Anti-masonic Pamphlets*, Harvard College Library,
No. 12, p. 18 ; *ib.* No. 9.

was brought up; taking an active part in
the services and the responses, and kneeling
in prayer, we are told, even when the pews
were so narrow that his tall form had to be
accommodated by the projection of his feet
into the aisle.  His friend, Bishop Meade,
the Episcopal bishop of Virginia, states that
he was never a communicant in that church;
and he quotes a letter from an Episcopal
clergyman who often visited Mrs. Harvie,
Marshall's only daughter, in her last illness,
and who reports from her the statement
that, during the last months of his life, he
told her " that the reason why he never
communed was that he was a Unitarian in
opinion, though he never joined their society."    It is added, however, in the same
letter, that Mrs. Harvie, a person " of the
strictest probity, the most humble piety, and
the most clear and discriminating mind,"
also said that, during these last months,
Marshall read Keith on Prophecy, and was
convinced by that work, and the fuller investigation to which it led, of the supreme
divinity of Jesus, and wished to commune,

but thought it his duty to do it publicly; and while waiting for the opportunity, died.

The reader of such a statement seems to perceive or to conjecture an anxiety to relieve the memory of the Chief Justice of an opprobrium.    Whatever the exact fact may be about this late change in opinion, there is little occasion to be surprised that Marshall shared, during his active life, the opinions of his friend Judge Story.    The genuineness and the simplicity of Marshall's lifelong piety are indicated by another statement reported from Mrs. Harvie : " Her father told her that he never went to bed without concluding his prayer with those which his mother taught him when a child, viz. the Lord's prayer and the prayer beginning, ' Now I lay me down to sleep.'"

Marshall was a man of vigorous physique. " He was always," says a descendant,[1] " devoted to walking, but more especially before breakfast in the early morning.    A venerable professor I met in Washington told me that, when he was a boy, regularly every morning

[1] Mrs. Hardy, 8 *Green Bag*, 487.

at seven o'clock, when he was on his way to
school, he met the Chief Justice returning
from a long walk. He walked rapidly always. Hon. Horace Binney says: ' After
doing my best one morning to overtake
Chief Justice Marshall, in his quick march
to the Capitol, when he was nearer to eighty
than seventy, I asked him to what cause in
particular he attributed that strong and
quick step, and he replied that he thought it
was most due to his commission in the army
of the Revolution, in which he had been a
regular foot practitioner for six years.' "

We often hear of the Chief Justice at his
" Quoit Club." He was a famous player at
quoits. A club had been formed by some
of the early Scotch settlers of Richmond,
and it came to include among its members
leading men of the city, such as Marshall,
Wirt, Nicholas, Call, Munford, and others.
Chester Harding, the artist who painted the
full-length portrait of Marshall that hangs
in the Boston Athenæum, tells us of seeing him at the Quoit Club. Fortunately,
language does not, like paint, limit the artist

to a single moment of time. He gives us
the Chief Justice in action. Marshall was
then attending the Virginia Constitutional
Convention, which sat from October, 1829,
to January, 1830. The Quoit Club used to
meet every week in a beautiful grove, about
a mile from the city. Harding went early.
" I watched," he says, " for the coming of
the old chief. He soon approached, with
his coat on his arm and his hat in his hand,
which he was using as a fan. He walked
directly up to a large bowl of mint julep,
which had been prepared, and drank off a
tumblerful of the liquid, smacking his lips,
and then turned to the company with a
cheerful 'How are you, gentlemen?' He
was looked upon as the best pitcher of the
party, and could throw heavier quoits than
any other member of the club. The game
began with great animation. There were
several ties; and before long I saw the great
Chief Justice of the United States down on
his knees, measuring the contested distance
with a straw, with as much earnestness as if
it had been a point of law; and if he proved

to be in the right, the woods would ring
with his triumphant shout." [1]

[1] In speaking of this same Club, Mr. G. W. Munford
says: " We have seen Mr. Marshall, in later times, when
he was Chief Justice of the United States, on his hands
and knees, with a straw and a penknife, the blade of the
knife stuck through the straw, holding it between the
edge of the quoit and the hub; and when it was a very
doubtful question, pinching or biting off the ends of the
straw, until it would fit to a hair."

James K. Paulding has preserved an entertaining account of a game, in 1820, when Jarvis, the artist, was
present, playing, apparently on the same side with the
Chief Justice.  " I remember," he says, " in the course of
the game, and when the parties were nearly at a tie, that
some dispute arose as to the quoit nearest the meg.  The
Chief Justice was chosen umpire between the quoit belonging to Jarvis and that of Billy Haxall.  The judge
bent down on one knee, and with a straw essayed the decision of this important question on which the fate of the
game in a great measure depended.  After nicely measuring, and frequently biting off the end of the straw,
' Gentlemen,' said he, ' you will perceive this quoit would
have it, but the rule of the game is to measure from the
visible iron.  Now that clod of dirt hides almost half an
inch.  But, then he has a right to the nearest part of the
meg; and here, as you will perceive, is a splinter, which
belongs to and is part of the meg, as much as the State
of Virginia is a part of the Union.  This is giving Mr.
Haxall a great advantage ; but, notwithstanding, in my
opinion, Jarvis has it by at least the sixteenth part of an
inch, and so I decide, like a just judge, in my own favor.' "
[2] *Lippincott's Magazine*, 623, 626.  It is said that he was
often appointed thus to be judge in his own case.

An entertaining account has been preserved [1] of a meeting of the club, held, apparently, while Marshall was still at the
bar, at which he and Wickham — a leading
Virginia lawyer, one of the counsel of Aaron
Burr — were the caterers.    At the table
Marshall announced that at the last meeting
two members had introduced politics, a forbidden subject, and had been fined a basket
of champagne, and that this was now produced, as a warning to evil-doers ; as the
club seldom drank this article, they had no
champagne glasses, and must drink it in
tumblers.    Those who played quoits retired,
after a while, for a game.    Most of the
members had smooth, highly polished brass
quoits.    But Marshall's were large, rough,
heavy, and of iron, such as few of the members could throw well from hub to hub.
Marshall himself threw them with great
success and accuracy, and often " rang the
meg."    On this occasion Marshall and the
Rev. Mr. Blair led the two parties of play-
ers.    Marshall played first, and rang the

[1] See *The Two Parsons*, by G. W. Munford.

meg. Parson Blair did the same, and his
quoit came down plumply on top of Marshall's. There was uproarious applause,
which drew out all the others from the dinner; and then came an animated controversy as to what should be the effect of this
exploit. They all returned to the table,
had another bottle of champagne, and listened to arguments, one from Marshall, *pro
se*, and one from Wickham for Parson Blair.
The company decided against Marshall. His
argument is a humorous companion piece to
any one of his elaborate judicial opinions.
He began by formulating the question,
" Who is winner when the adversary quoits
are on the meg at the same time? " He
then stated the facts, and remarked that the
question was one of the true construction
and application of the rules of the game.
The one first ringing the meg has the advantage. No other can succeed who does
not begin by displacing this first one. The
parson, he willingly allowed, deserves to rise
higher and higher in everybody's esteem;
but then he must n't do it by getting on

another's back in this fashion. That is more like leapfrog than quoits. Then, again, the legal maxim is, *Cujus est solum, ejus est usque ad cœlum*, — his own right as first occupant extends to the vault of heaven; no opponent can gain any advantage by squatting on his back. He must either bring a writ of ejectment, or drive him out *vi et armis*. And then, after further argument of the same sort, he asked judgment, and sat down amidst great applause.

Mr. Wickham then rose, and made an argument of a similar pattern. No rule, he said, requires an impossibility. Mr. Marshall's quoit is twice as large as any other; and yet it flies from his arm like the iron ball at the Grecian games from the arm of Ajax. It is an iron quoit, unpolished, jagged, and of enormous weight. It is impossible for an ordinary quoit to move it. With much more of the same sort, he contended that it was a drawn game. After very animated voting, designed to keep up the uncertainty as long as possible, it was so decided. Another trial was had, and Marshall clearly won.

All his life he played this game. There
is an account of a country barbecue in the
mountain region, where a casual guest saw
him, then an old man, emerge from a thicket
which bordered a brook, carrying a pile of
flat stones as large as he could hold between
his right arm and his chin. He stepped
briskly up to the company and threw them
down. "There! Here are quoits enough
for us all."

Of Marshall's simple habits, remarkable
modesty, and engaging simplicity of conduct and demeanor, every one who knew him
speaks. These things were in the grain,
and outlasted all the wear and tear of life.
"What was it in him which most impressed
you?" asked one of his descendants, now a
distinguished judge,[1] of an older relative who
had known him. "His humility," was her
answer. "With Marshall," wrote President
Quincy, "I had considerable acquaintance
during the eight years I was member of
Congress, from 1805 to 1813, played chess

[1] Mr. Justice Keith, now President of the Virginia
Court of Appeals.

with him, and never failed to be impressed
with the frank, cordial, childlike simplicity
and unpretending manner of the man, of
whose strength and breadth of intellectual
power I was . . . well apprised."

"Nothing was more usual," we are told,
as regards his life in Richmond, "than to
see him returning from market, at sunrise,
with poultry in one hand and a basket of
vegetables in the other." And, again, some
one speaks of meeting him on horseback, at
sunrise, with a bag of seeds before him, on
his way to his farm, three or four miles out
of town. It was of this farm that he wrote
to James Monroe, his old friend and schoolmate, about passing so much time in "*laborious relaxation.*" The italics are his own.

In speaking of Marshall's personal qualities and ways, I must quote from those exquisite passages in Judge Story's address,
delivered in the fall of 1835, to the Suffolk
bar, in which his own true affection found
expression: "Upon a first introduction he
would be thought to be cold and reserved;
but he was neither the one nor the other. It

was simply a habit of easy taciturnity, watching, as it were, his own turn to follow the line of conversation, and not to presume to lead it. . . . Meet him in a stage-coach as a stranger, and travel with him a whole day, and you would only be struck with his readiness to administer to the accommodation of others, and his anxiety to appropriate least to himself. Be with him the unknown guest at an inn, and he seemed adjusted to the very scene; partaking of the warm welcome of its comforts, whenever found; and if not found, resigning himself without complaint to its meanest arrangements. . . . He had great simplicity of character, manners, dress, and deportment, and yet with a natural dignity that suppressed impertinence and silenced rudeness. His simplicity . . . had an exquisite naïveté, which charmed every one, and gave a sweetness to his familiar conversation approaching to fascination. The first impression of a stranger, upon his introduction to him, was generally that of disappointment. It seemed hardly credible that such simplicity should be the accompaniment

of such acknowledged greatness. The con-
sciousness of power was not there; the air
of office was not there; there was no play of
the lights or shades of rank, no study of effect
in tone or bearing."

Add to this what Judge Story said from
the bench, in receiving the resolutions of
the Bar of the Supreme Court after Marshall's death: "But, above all, he was the
ornament of human nature itself, in the
beautiful illustrations which his life con-
stantly presented, of its most attractive
graces, and its most elevated attributes." [1]

Of Marshall's appearance on the bench we
have a picture in one of Story's letters from
Washington, while he was at the bar. He
is writing in 1808, the year after the Burr
trial. "Marshall," he says, "is of a tall,
slender figure, not graceful or imposing, but
erect and steady. His hair is black, his eyes
small and twinkling, his forehead rather low,
but his features are in general harmonious.
His manners are plain, yet dignified; and an
unaffected modesty diffuses itself through all

[1] 10 Peters's Reports, vii.

his actions.  His dress is very simple, yet neat; his language chaste, but hardly elegant; it does not flow rapidly, but it seldom wants precision.  In conversation he is quite familiar, but is occasionally embarrassed by a hesitancy and drawling. . . . I love his laugh, — it is too hearty for an intriguer, — and his good temper and unwearied patience are equally agreeable on the bench and in the study."

Daniel Webster, in 1814, while he was a member of Congress from New Hampshire, wrote to his brother: " There is no man in the court that strikes me like Marshall.  He is a plain man, looking very much like Colonel Adams, and about three inches taller.  I have never seen a man of whose intellect I had a higher opinion."

In the year 1808, when Judge Story wrote what has just been quoted, Marshall was sketched in chalk by St. Mémin.  It is a beautiful portrait, which its present owner, Mr. Thomas Marshall Smith, of Baltimore, John Marshall's great-grandson, has now generously allowed to be copied for the use of the public.

It was in 1830 that Chester Harding
painted for the Boston Athenæum the full-
length portrait, of which, a little later, he
made the replica, afterwards purchased, by
subscription, for the Harvard Law School.
" I consider it," says Harding, " a good picture.[1]   I had great pleasure in painting *the
whole* of such a man. . . . When I was ready
to draw the figure into his picture, I asked
him, in order to save time, to come to my
room in the evening. . . . An evening was appointed ; but he could not come until after the
' consultation,' which lasts until about eight
o'clock."    It will be remembered that the
judges, at that time, used to lodge together,
in one house.   " It was a warm evening," continues Harding, " and I was standing on my
steps waiting for him, when he soon made his
appearance, but, to my surprise, without a hat.
I showed him into my studio, and stepped

---

[1] The half-length, sitting portrait of Marshall, in the
dining-hall at Cambridge, was painted by Harding, in
1828, for the Chief Justice himself ; and by him given to
Judge Story, " to be preserved, when I shall sleep with
my fathers, as a testimonial of sincere and affectionate
friendship."   Story bequeathed it to the college.

back to fasten the front door, when I en-
countered [several gentlemen] who knew the
judge very well.   They had seen him passing
by their hotel in his hatless condition, and
with long strides, as if in great haste, and
had followed, curious to know the cause of
such a strange appearance. . . . He said that
the consultation lasted longer than he expected, and he hurried off as quickly as possible to keep his appointment with me."   He
declined the offer of a hat on his return :
" Oh no, it is a warm night ; I shall not need
one."

A good many artists tried their hands on
the Chief Justice, and with every sort of
result.   Some depicted a dull and wooden
person, some a worthy but feeble one.   Other
portraits, commended for their likeness to
the original, differ much in what they repre-
sent.[1]

[1] See an interesting article by Mr. Justice Bradley, of
the Supreme Court of the United States, on portraits of
Marshall, in the *Century Magazine* for September, 1889,
(vol. 38, page 778.)   A portrait by Jarvis, valued as a
work of art and as a good likeness, is in the possession of
Mr. Justice Gray.   Mr. Justice Bradley appears to be

In the written descriptions of him, also, one needs to compare several before he can feel much assurance of the true image. In an anonymous account of him, preserved in Van Santvoord's "Lives of the Chief Justices,"[1] the reader seems to perceive the humorous exaggerations of an entertaining and practiced writer, but, taken with due allowance, the description may well be preserved.

"As to face and figure," says this account, "nature had been equally little at pains to stamp, with any princely effigy of what pleases, the virgin gold of which she had composed his head and heart. Except that his countenance was thoughtful and benignant, it had nothing about it that would have commanded a second look. Separately his features were but indifferent, jointly they were no more than commonplace. Then as to stature, shape, and carriage, there was

wrong in saying that there is a full-length of Marshall at Washington and Lee University. There are two portraits of him there, but, as I am assured, no full-length.

[1] P. 363, n.

nothing in him that was not the opposite of commanding or prepossessing; he was tall, yet his height was without the look of either strength or lightness, and gave neither dignity nor grace.  His body seemed as ill as his mind well compacted; he not only was without proportion, but of members singularly knit, that dangled from each other and looked half dislocated.  Habitually he dressed very carelessly; in the garb, I should not dare to say in the mode, of the last century. You would have thought he had on the old clothes of a former generation, not made for him by even some superannuated tailor of the period, but gotten from the wardrobe of some antiquated slop-shop of second-hand raiment.  Shapeless as he was, he would probably have defied all fitting, by whatever skill of the shears; judge then how the vestments of an age when, apparently, coats and breeches were cut for nobody in particular, and waistcoats were almost dressing gowns, sat upon him."

Such a statement should be supplemented by what one of his family said of him : " The

descriptions of his dress are greatly exagger-
ated ; he was regardless of style and fashion,
but all those who knew him best testified to
the extreme neatness of his attire." [1]

[1] Mrs. Hardy, quoting her grandmother, in 8 *Green
Bag*, 484.

## CHAPTER VIII

THE year 1831 was a sad one for Marshall. The greatest apprehensions were felt for his health. " Wirt," says John Quincy Adams in his diary, on February 13, 1831, " spoke to me, also, in deep concern and alarm at the state of Chief Justice Marshall's health." In the autumn he went to Philadelphia to undergo the torture of the operation of lithotomy, before the days of ether. It was the last operation performed by the distinguished surgeon, Dr. Physick. Another eminent surgeon, who assisted him, Dr. Randall, has given an account of this occasion, in which he says : —

" It will be readily admitted that, in consequence of Judge Marshall's very advanced age, the hazard attending the operation, however skillfully performed, was considerably increased. I consider it but an act of

justice, due to the memory of that great and
good man, to state that, in my opinion, his
recovery was in a great degree owing to his
extraordinary self-possession, and to the
calm and philosophical views which he took
of his case, and the various circumstances
attending it.

"It fell to my lot to make the necessary
preparations. In the discharge of this duty
I visited him on the morning of the day
fixed on for the operation, two hours previously to that at which it was to be performed. Upon entering his room I found
him engaged in eating his breakfast. He
received me with a pleasant smile upon his
countenance, and said: 'Well, doctor, you
find me taking breakfast, and I assure you I
have had a good one. I thought it very
probable that this might be my last chance,
and therefore I determined to enjoy it and
eat heartily.' I expressed the great pleasure which I felt at seeing him so cheerful, and said that I hoped all would soon be
happily over. He replied to this that he
did not feel the least anxiety or uneasiness

respecting the operation or its results. He said that he had not the slightest desire to live, laboring under the sufferings to which he was then subjected; that he was perfectly ready to take all the chances of an operation, and he knew there were many against him; and that if he could be relieved by it he was willing to live out his appointed time, but if not, would rather die than hold existence accompanied with the pain and misery which he then endured.

"After he finished his breakfast I administered to him some medicine; he then inquired at what hour the operation would be performed. I mentioned the hour of eleven. He said, 'Very well, do you wish me now for any other purpose, or may I lie down and go to sleep?' I was a good deal surprised at this question, but told him that if he could sleep it would be very desirable. He immediately placed himself upon the bed, and fell into a profound sleep, and continued so until I was obliged to rouse him in order to undergo the operation. He exhibited the same fortitude, scarcely uttering a murmur,

throughout the whole procedure, which, from
the peculiar nature of his complaint, was
necessarily tedious."

From the patient over a thousand calculi
were taken. He had a perfect recovery;
nor did the disorder ever return.[1]

On Christmas Day of that year, as I have
said, his wife died, the object of his tender-
est affection ever since he had first seen her,
more than fifty years before. The day before she died, she hung about his neck a
locket with some of her hair. He wore it
always, night and day; and, by his order,
it was the last thing removed from his body
when he died.[2]

It was at this period, in 1831 and 1832,

[1] My friend Dr. Horace Howard Furness, of Philadelphia, writes (and allows me to quote) : " I remember
hearing my father say that Dr. Physick told him, just
after that operation of lithotomy, that he had ' washed
the judge out as clean as a plate,' and that he went on
to say that after the operation the strictest quiet was en-
joined, not a muscle was to be moved; but what was his
alarm on his next visit to see Judge Marshall sitting up
in bed with paper and pencil on his knees, writing to his
wife ! "

[2] Marion Harland, *Old Colonial Homesteads*, 98.

that Inman's fine portrait of him, now hang-
ing in the rooms of the Law Association
of Philadelphia, was painted, for the bar of
that city.   A replica which Marshall himself bought for his daughter, is on the walls
of the state library in Richmond.   This portrait is regarded as the best of those painted
in his later life.   Certainly it best answers
the description of him by an English traveler, who, seeing him often in the spring
of 1835, remarked that "the venerable
dignity of his appearance would not suffer
in comparison with that of the most respected and distinguished-looking peer in
the British House of Lords." [1]

After his recovery, in 1831, Marshall
seems to have been in good health down to
the early part of 1835.   Then, we are told,
he suffered "severe contusions" in the
stage-coach in returning from Washington.[2]

[1] *Travels in North America*, by Hon. Charles Augustus
Murray, — "the late Sir Charles Murray, at one time
Master of the Household to the Queen, who, as a young
man, was attached to the British Legation at Washington."
— *The Spectator*, February 9, 1901, p. 199.

[2] Many a "severe contusion" must he have suffered in

His health now rapidly declined. He went
again for relief to Philadelphia, and died
there on July 6, 1835, of a serious disorder
of the liver. He had missed from his bed-
side his oldest son, Thomas, for whom he
had been asking. Upon the gravestone of
that son, behind the old house at Oakhill,
you may read the pathetic tragedy, withheld
from his father, that accounts for this ab-
sence. While hastening to Philadelphia, at
the end of June, he was passing through the
streets of Baltimore, in the midst of a tem-
pest, and was killed by the falling of a
chimney in the storm.

The great Chief Justice was carried home
with every demonstration of respect and
reverence. He was buried by the side of

those primitive days, from upsets and joltings, in driving
every year between Richmond and Washington, some
120 miles each way; from Richmond to Raleigh and
back, in attending his North Carolina circuit, about 175
miles each way; and between Richmond and Oakhill,
his country place, every summer, about 100 miles each
way. For instance, in 1812, Cranch, the reporter, remarks that Marshall was not present at the beginning of
the term, as he " received an injury by the oversetting
of the stage-coach on his journey from Richmond."

his wife, in the Shockoe Hill Cemetery in
Richmond.    There, upon horizontal tablets,
are two inscriptions of affecting simplicity,
both written by himself.    The first runs
thus : " John Marshall, Son of Thomas and
Mary Marshall, was born the 24th of September, 1755.    Intermarried with Mary
Willis Ambler, the 3d of January, 1783.
Departed this life the [6th] day of July,
1835."    The second, thus : " Sacred to the
memory of Mrs. Mary Willis Marshall,
Consort of John Marshall, Born the 13th of
March, 1766.    Departed this life the 25th of
December, 1831.    This stone is devoted to
her memory by him who best knew her
worth, And most deplores her loss."

Among the tributes to Chief Justice
Marshall which were made in the months
that followed his death, and in later times,
nothing finer has been said than the heart-
felt expression of the bar of his own circuit,
at Richmond, in November, 1835.    The
resolutions of Mr. B. Watkins Leigh, unani-
mously adopted, recalled " the memory of

the venerable judge " who had presided there
for more than thirty-four years "with such
remarkable diligence in office, that until he
was disabled by the disease which removed
him from life, he was never known to be ab-
sent from the bench, during term time, even
for a day, — with such indulgence to counsel and suitors that everybody's convenience
was consulted but his own, — with a dignity, sustained without effort, and apparently without care to sustain it, to which
all men were solicitous to pay due respect, —
with such profound sagacity, such quick pene-
tration, such acuteness, clearness, strength,
and comprehension of mind, that in his
hands the most complicated causes were
plain, the weightiest and most difficult, easy
and light, — with such striking impartiality
and justice, and a judgment so sure, as to
inspire universal confidence, so that few appeals were ever taken from his decisions,
during his long administration of justice in
this court, and those only in cases where he
himself expressed doubt, — with such modesty that he seemed wholly unconscious of

his own gigantic powers, — with such equa-
nimity, such benignity of temper, such amen-
ity of manners, that not only none of the
judges who sat with him on the bench, but
no member of the bar, no officer of the
court, no juror, no witness, no suitor, in a
single instance, ever found or imagined, in
anything said or done, or omitted by him,
the slightest cause of offense.

" His private life was worthy of the ex-
alted character he sustained in public station. The unaffected simplicity of his manners ; the spotless purity of his morals ; his
social, gentle, cheerful, disposition ; his
habitual self-denial, and boundless gener-
osity towards others; the strength and con-
stancy of his attachments, his kindness to
his friends and neighbors; his exemplary
conduct in the relations of son, brother, hus-
band, father; his numerous charities; his
benevolence toward all men, and his ever
active beneficence; these amiable qualities
shone so conspicuously in him, throughout
his life, that highly as he was respected,
he had the rare happiness to be yet more

beloved.   He was, indeed, a bright example
of the true wisdom which consists in the
union of the greatest ability and the greatest virtue."

On the west side of the Capitol at Washington, midway between the staircases that
ascend from the garden to the great building, and a little in advance, there is a colos-
sal bronze figure of Marshall by the sculptor
Story, the son of the great man's colleague
and friend, — placed there in 1884.   It is a
very noble work of art, worthy of the subject and the place.   The Chief Justice is
sitting, clothed in his judicial robe, in the
easy attitude of one engaged in expounding
a subject of which he is master.   The figure is leaning back in the chair with the
head slightly inclining forward ; the right
arm rests on the arm of the chair, with the
hand open and extended ; the left hand,
holding a scroll, lies easily on the other arm
of the chair.   The crossed legs are covered
by the gown, while low shoes and buckles,
and hair gathered in a queue, speak of life-

long habits. The solid and beautiful head, and the grave and collected dignity of the features and the whole composition are very noble, satisfactory, and ideally true.

The figure, standing, would be ten feet high. It sits seven feet high, and is raised upon a suitable pedestal, decorated with marble bas-reliefs of classical designs. These, if the truth were told, might well be spared, but the statue itself will fitly commemorate for many ages one of the greatest, noblest and most engaging characters in American history.

**The Riverside Press**
*Electrotyped and printed by H. O. Houghton & Co.*
*Cambridge, Mass., U. S. A.*